Tashia Stuart & Other Stories A Collection of True Crime

Sarah Thompson

Published by Trellis Publishing, 2021.

While every precaution has been taken in the preparation of this book, the publisher assumes no responsibility for errors or omissions, or for damages resulting from the use of the information contained herein.

TASHIA STUART & OTHER STORIES A COLLECTION OF TRUE CRIME

First edition. July 1, 2021.

ISBN: 979-8224351664

Written by Sarah Thompson.

TASHIA STUART : KILLER

Sarah Thomerson

1

"Paranoid" is the term often ascribed to those who believe that others are out to get them. Society doesn't tend to take these fears seriously, especially when it comes from someone who doesn't lead a dangerous life. After all, there aren't many people who can definitively say that there are people plotting to do them great harm. But for one Washington woman, the gut feeling that someone was planning her death was more than just paranoia. In fact, it was intuition. Unfortunately, it was familial loyalties and ties that kept her from acting on that intuition in order to stop the grim tragedy that was about to unfold.

Long before the fateful afternoon of March 3rd, 2011, a woman by the name of Judy Herbert spoke to her ex-husband, as well as several of her friends, and expressed worry and fear that her daughter was trying to kill her. It seemed that in the weeks leading up to March 3rd, Judy Herbert would tell anyone who would listen that something was amiss in her life and that it was her daughter who was behind it. To some, these worries might have felt blown out of proportion. After all, what would drive someone's adult daughter to murder them?

The story begins long before 2011, in California. Judy Herbert and former husband Rolfe Herbert brought Tashia into their home when she was just six months old. Born in 1970, Tashia was the daughter of Judy's twin sister, Jody. Unfortunately, Jody wasn't living a life fit for raising a little girl. Jody had issues that made being a mother difficult for her. As a prostituted woman, Jody suffered from the trauma and psychological issues. She lived in a world that wasn't conducive to raising a child in a safe and healthy manner.

Jody gave up Tashia to Judy, and like any good family would, Judy stepped up to be a mother for Tashia. In Rolfe's own words, he was "elated" to have Tashia in his life. All in all, Tashia was lucky that her mother had a sister who could step in and care for her. Many children born to prostituted women suffer disappearing into the system- or worse, the streets. From the moment Tashia entered their home, Judy and Rolfe loved her as if she was their own biological daughter. And while Judy may not have given birth to her, Tashia was never treated as if she was anything less than their biological child.

While Judy adored Tashia from the moment she adopted her, the feeling did not grow to be mutual. As Tashia got older, she got more and more troublesome. More than just entering her unruly teenager phase, Tashia began to express nothing short of hatred towards her mother. In 1988, living in Fresno, California, 15-year-old Tashia was getting into trouble on what seemed like a daily basis. Like most teenagers, Tashia was testing her boundaries. However, there seemed to be something inside of her that wasn't in other teenager girls.

As a young child, and into her teenage years, Tashia couldn't seem to stop lying. According to her father, Rolfe Herbert, Tashia always got in trouble for lying. It seemed that it didn't matter how big or small the situation was, Tashia would lie about it anyway. "If she broke a glass," Rolfe Herbert spoke in an interview, about young Tashia. "It was somebody else's fault. Something else happened. She didn't do it."

Tashia began to sneak out of her home as a teenager. Rolfe Herbert would often have to report to the police that she ran away in order to find some way to bring her home. "It was non-stop," Rolfe dismayed. While Tashia's teenage ire was directly mostly at her mother, she would often tell Rolfe as well that neither of them were her "real parents". When she got older, into her late teenage years, Tashia took her constant running away one step further. She left for good. Or at least, that was the intention.

But Tashia didn't leave her adopted family behind. In fact, according to Rolfe Herbert, he and Judy saw Tashia on a regular basis whenever she needed something from them. If she was facing a night on the street, Tashia would come to them for a place to spend the night. If she was running low on funds, Tashia would find Judy and Rolfe and ask them for money. Despite her how much Tashia claimed she didn't like her adoptive parents, and how much she didn't need them, Tashia would always come running back when she needed their support.

For the length of her adult life, Tashia would come in and out of Judy and Rolfe's life, even after the two divorced. In January 2011, Tashia found herself returning to Judy, seeking help. By then, Judy had moved to Pasco, Washington. Tashia was in serious debt and had no money to her name. She needed help, and she went to the mother she had long scorned, who had always been there to help her when she needed it. By then, Tashia was 41 years old and had a husband of her own by the name of Todd, and seven-year-old daughter.

Despite all the trouble that Tashia had caused Judy during her younger years, Judy still thought herself Tashia's mother. She extended the invitation to Tashia and her family to move in with her while they got their lives back together. For Tashia, this was a second chance that many people didn't get in their lives. For Judy, this was an opportunity for her to be able to spend some much-needed quality time with her young granddaughter.

According to Rolfe, Judy loved that little girl more than anything. As Rolfe put it, "she was the center of her [Judy's] world." However, no long after Tashia moved her family into Judy's Washington home, tension sprang up throughout the house between the two of them. Of course, money was one of the things that caused an even bigger rift to grow between Tashia and her adopted mother.

Wanting to help them out with their financial struggles, Judy had given Tashia a debit card that was connected to her own bank account. The understanding was that Tashia would only use it to purchase things that she needed from the store, such as food, or things for her daughter. Instead, Tashia saw it as a free-for-all. She began taking hundreds of dollars from Judy's account, stealing money from her even when Judy had opened her home (and her bank account) to help her daughter and granddaughter.

Despite it all, Judy continued to let Tashia and her family stay with her in her home. After all, to those who knew Judy, she was incredibly kind and caring. She would have done anything to make sure that her granddaughter was getting the life she deserved, even if it meant putting up with Tashia sneaking around and stealing money from her. Perhaps Judy saw in Tashia that she had seen in her own sister: a mother who wasn't prepared to give the child she bore what she needed in life.

Perhaps Judy also saw a little of Tashia in her granddaughter - or rather, she saw the child she had hoped to raise out of Tashia. Maybe, to Judy, this was a second chance at doing motherhood the right way. To those who knew her, there was very little that Judy would do for her granddaughter, even if that meant putting up with the sinking suspicion that Tashia wanted to do her a great deal of harm.

A little over two months into Tashia and her family's stay with Judy, something went horribly wrong. On February 20th, 2011, Tashia's husband, Todd Stuart, came to Judy and asked her to assist him with taking measurements of her garage floor. Todd wanted to build a wall in the garage. When he handed her the measuring tape, he held onto one end while Judy held onto the other. Todd instructed Judy to back up with the measuring tape, and only stopped when he told her to.

From above, in the rafters of the garage, something heavy fell from the ceiling. It was an 18-gallon tub that was, at the time, filled to the brim with books. It's such a heavy drop that it threw Judy to the ground, and it was near miss to breaking her neck. Tashia called her father, Rolfe, who was now Judy's ex-husband. Despite the divorce, Judy and Rolfe stayed close. According to Rolfe, they were still best friends.

However, when Tashia called her father to inform him of her mother's accident, she had a rather strange request. She told Rolfe that there had been an accident in the garage... but rather than asking him to come quickly, or even calling 911 herself, Tashia demanded the combination to the safe inside Judy Herbert's home that held her mother's will, along with the "do not resuscitate" order. Rolfe found that to be strange, as well. Rather than giving it over, he told Tashia that she didn't need "any of that stuff", and that she needed to have up and dial emergency services right away.

However, Tashia answered, "Mom won't let me."

Thankfully, Judy hadn't been knocked unconscious from the blow to the head, nor had she been seriously injured. When Tashia put Rolfe on the phone with her, Judy told Rolfe that she felt rather awful, but that she wasn't sure she needed to be taken to the hospital. That should have been the end of it. However, Rolfe received two more phone calls from Tashia that same day, continuing to ask for the combination to the safe. Each time, Rolfe refused.

According to Rolfe, Tashia told him, "[...] Everything in that safe is mine anyway." To which, Rolfe replied, "Then ask mom for the combination." After that, Tashia didn't call again for the combination. But, it still left a foul taste in everyone's mouth.

It wasn't long after the accident in the garage that Tashia spoke to her ex-boyfriend, Charles Adney, who also happened to be the father of her young daughter. She began to ask him worrying questions—such as, would he be willing to be a witness on a forged will? According to Tashia, she wanted to make sure that she was the only person who would get anything from Judy Herbert's will if she were to die. During that same conversation, she told Charles that Judy "would be dead soon", and joked about using something "round" instead of "flat" when it came to dropping an object on Judy's head.

It was around this same time that Judy first began to grow suspicious of her daughter and began speaking to friends, as well as her ex-husband, Rolfe, about how she feared that perhaps Tashia was planning on killing her. Judy relayed these fears to her neighbor, Deborah Severin. She even went so far as to asking Severin if she would come and check on her on Mondays if Tashia and Todd were home with her over the weekend.

Judy's fear of Tashia and Todd was so great that she and Severin came up with a code word. If Judy felt that she needed Severin to contact the police, but feared for her life if Tashia knew, she would tell Severin the word "lavender" in conversation. This would alert her neighbor that Judy needed help, and to call the police to come to her home as soon as possible. By this time, Judy suspected that Tashia had been hiding in the rafters in order to drop the tub of books on her head.

Judy told this theory to another neighbor, Ryan Rhodes, and told him that if she were ever to be away from her home for any length of time, that it would mean Tashia and Todd had disposed of her body in the backyard. The fear, for Judy Herbert, was more than just paranoia. It was incredibly real, and she felt for certain that an attempt on her life had already been made. But Severin and Rhodes weren't the only neighbors that Judy had relayed her fear too. Judy spoke with yet another neighbor, this one by the name of Tonya Amende, about the incident in the garage. Judy also spoke with Amende about how she was worried that her daughter and son-in-law were, as she described it, "messing with her medication". With each passing day, Judy was more and more convinced of the idea that Tashia and Todd had planned to kill her that day, but didn't succeed.

Judy had a diagram of the garage, pictures of the truck and the rafters, and felt certain that someone had climbed up into the rafters in order to push the tub of books on her head. She told Amende that the truck looked as if someone had stood on it in order to climb up into the ceiling of her garage. The diagram she drew showed where Todd had her stand relative to the open floor of the rafters where the books fell. Judy hid all of this evidence in her safe.

On March 2nd, 2011, Judy Herbert made a call to her banker, Toni Capaul. She wanted to discuss some activity on her bank account that she hadn't made in the form of a retail purchase, as well as two cash withdrawals. While she canceled her debit card so that she could order a new one, she admitted to Capaul that she feared her son-in-law, Todd, was trying to kill her. She even told him about the books falling on her head from the garage. Judy Herbert's fear was real, and it was more than just paranoid ramblings.

Something terrible was going to happen to Judy Herbert, and she knew it. Not only did her friends and neighbors hear Judy's fears, but so did her best friend and ex-husband, Rolfe Herbert. She told Rolfe that she feared Tashia and Todd were screwing around with her medication, as well as the suspicious activity on her bank account.

On March 3rd, 2011, Rolfe received a phone call from Tashia. She and Judy always seemed to be having disputes and problems in the household. Rolfe was on the receiving end of many of Tashia's complaints about Judy. That day, Tashia called and asked, "If mom comes home, what do I do?" Of course, Rolfe's response was that Tashia should leave the house if she was having problems with her mother. He even insisted that Judy had trouble walking, and even raising her arms and that she was no threat to Tashia.

Perhaps it was this sentiment that inspired Tashia to do what she did. After all, Judy was no threat to her... which meant that she couldn't defend herself against Tashia.

At 2:25 pm on March 3rd, a 911 call reached the Franklin County Sheriff's dispatch, but whoever had been on the other line had hung up. When calling back, a woman (most likely Tashia) picked up the phone and answered that it was a false alarm due to a fire alarm going off while the batteries were being changed.

Within a few minutes of that 911 call, Ryan Rhodes was outside his home working on his car. The sound of gunshots rang through the air, coming right from Judy Herbert's house. After hearing one shot, Rhodes looked over to the home and could see the window panes of the house shudder with the force of two more gunshots. Rhodes immediately went inside and phoned over to Judy Herbert's house. Of course, it was Tashia who picked up the phone. He told Tashia that he wanted to make sure that Judy was alright, and asked to speak to her.

Tashia's excuse for the sounds of the gunshots was that something had exploded on the stove and that her mother was lying down and didn't want to be disturbed. To Rhodes, this sounded suspicious. Instead of taking Tashia for her word, Rhodes did the right thing and hurried over to another neighbor's house, Tonya Amende. Rhodes asked Amende to call over to Judy's house and check in on her. When Amende called, it was once more Tashia who answered the phone. She gave the same excuses about the stove but slipped up when she said that her mother was in the bathroom throwing up, rather than lying down and sleeping. Amende asked Tashia to have Judy call her back when she could, and Tashia replied that she would.

Meanwhile, the 911 call hadn't gone ignored, even when told that it was a mistake because of the fire alarm. Officer Kevin Erickson showed up at Judy Herbert's house in the wake of the 911 call, about 10 minutes after the initial call, and the sound of gunshots heard by the neighbors. When Officer Erickson knocked on the door, Tashia answered, looking harried and upset. Tashia told the officer that something had exploded on the stove and that her mother was sick in the bathroom.

Officer Erickson asked if he could come in and talk about what was going on. After all, Tashia seemed rather upset, and there had been concerning noises from the house. Tashia agreed, but only after she could put the dogs in another room. She shut the front door again and left Officer Erickson to wait outside. To the officer, the wait felt "unusual". While he was waiting, Rhodes saw him from across the street and waved him over. Officer Erickson went, and the two spoke about what Rhodes had heard, and the phone calls he and Amende made and the suspicions that he had. After all, Judy Herbert had been telling everyone who would listen that she feared for her life around Tashia and Todd.

It seemed like those fears were finally coming to fruition.

Officer Erickson unclasped the holster of his gun, and make his way back towards Judy Herbert's house while he called for backup. As he was coming up the driveway, Tashia returned in the doorway. According to Officer Erickson, Tashia "flung" the door open and immediately said, "She came at me with an ax!"

Officer Dean Perry arrived for backup while Officer Erickson followed Tashia inside. She admitted that she had shot "someone" in the house, and the two officers followed her through the house. Officer Perry stopped in the living room, and stayed with Tashia's young daughter, while Officer Erickson followed Tashia to the bedroom. Judy Herbert was laying in the doorway of the bedroom. She had no pulse. Beside her, there was what looked to be a utility hatchet laying on the floor.

What exactly had happened inside that house during that grim March afternoon? When Tashia was taken in for questioning, she told detectives that she had woken up to Judy Herbert screaming at her about withdrawals from the bank account. Tashia said that Judy was furious about the "unauthorized withdrawals". Tashia claimed that she "reminded" her mother that she had given her a debit card to use, but claimed that her mother "didn't believe her". Tashia told detectives that Judy called Rolfe that morning and told him she was going to have Todd arrested.

Todd Stuart had moved out of the house two days previous, according to Tashia. She told detectives that she was trying to calm her mother down, while also making sure that Todd hadn't taken any important documents with him that she may need. So, Tashia said that she asked her mother to open up the safe so that she could check. In the layout of the house, the safe was located in a closet inside her mother's bedroom. While her mother opened the safe, Tashia said that she turned around with the utility hatchet in her hand and tried to swing it at her.

Tashia told detectives that's when she hid in the closet and found her mother's revolver that was inside the safe. When she returned to the bedroom with the gun, Tashia claimed that Judy Herbert was coming at her with the utility hatchet in hand, swinging it at her. In self-defense, Tashia claimed to have shot her adoptive mother until she fell to the floor. According to Tashia, when Judy fell, the utility hatchet also fell and struck her in the head.

Detectives were wary of Tashia Stuart's story. There were many inconsistencies- such as why she never mentioned this to the 911 dispatcher, and the conflicting stories she told the neighbors, and her demeanor when Officer Erickson first knocked on her door. If Tashia had been shooting her mother in self-defense and fear for her life, then why did she lock her daughter in a separate room and turn the volume of the television up so that she couldn't hear what was happening in another part of the house?

Tashia's story became unraveled with the information one of the detective's received about where Judy Herbert kept her revolver. It wasn't in the safe in the closet, but rather in her truck. Tashia often borrowed Judy's truck and knew where she kept her revolver. For Tashia to have it during the altercation meant that she had to have grabbed it, purposefully, from the truck. Evidence from the crime scene supported this theory since the case from the revolver was found behind the couch in the living room.

It only took a couple of days before Tashia was being charged with first-degree murder, along with attempted first-degree murder for the incident in the garage of February 20th. Tashia's story of what had happened inside the home on March 3rd wasn't all that it seemed. Strangely enough, it would be her own daughter that signed Tashia's downfall. While the name of Tashia's daughter has been kept from the public record for her own safety, court documents gave her simply the initial, S.

S. gave information to the detectives about what happened that day in the home. According to her, S. had learned how to open up the safe, most likely from all the time she spent with her grandmother. It was then that S. showed Tashia how to open up the safe, and when Tashia did so, she took all of the money out of it. It wasn't long before Judy Herbert found out that Tashia had stolen from her, and more than just strange withdrawals and purchases of her debit card. When Judy Herbert had found out that safe had been opened, and Tashia had taken the money from inside, she went to call the police.

That had been the 911 call, and Tashia had shot her mother in an attempt to keep her from reporting what she had done. The trial lasted for a month, and evidence showed that only two shots had managed to hit Judy, the fatal blow being a bullet that passed through a folder she had been holding, her thumb, and her chest cavity before striking her spinal column. Other evidence gathered from the home included hidden cameras in the closet in an attempt to catch Judy Herbert putting in the combination, as well as internet searches on how to open and crack safes.

In the end, the jury found Tashia Stuart guilty of first-degree murder and attempted first-degree murder of Judy Herbert. She was sentenced to 540 months in prison. Despite all of the evidence, Tashia claimed that it was her mother's drinking and medication that lead to Tashia shooting her that afternoon. She spoke for nearly 15 minutes about how Judy's mental health caused so many problems in her life, and how she missed her dearly and loved her. Tashia accused Judy Herbert of having fits of rage and accused Rolfe Herbert of conspiring against her and lying in order to put her behind bars for good.

Tashia was ordered a 25 minimum sentence out of the 45 years she would serve.

Tashia Stuart's greed ruined more than just Judy Herbert's life on March 3rd, 2011. Tashia's actions disrupted the life of her child, as well as all of Judy Herbert's friends and family members. Her request for appeal was denied, and Tashia Stuart is still behind bars where she belongs for the travesty that she unfolded onto her family.

JASMINE RICHARDSON

GERTRUDE SCOTT

On the South Saskatchewan River in Alberta, Canada is a town called Medicine Hat. With a population of just over 60,000 it is filled with little communities where everybody knows everybody. With a relatively low crime rate and virtually none of those crimes involving homicide it's the perfect place to raise a family in a safe environment, or at least it would seem that way I should I say. The security offered by Medicine Hat was greatly diminished when the entire town was shaken to its core in April of 2006.

On April 23, 2006 the community was rocked to its very foundation with the discovery of a gruesome triple homicide. An entire family was found stabbed to death in their home that day. The bodies were discovered by the 8 year old boy's best friend when he arrived at the house to get his friend to come out and play. When cops were notified and an investigation began the scene revealed was one of the worst scenes in Canadian history. Debra Richardson, 48 and her husband Marc, 42 were found in the basement with multiple stab wounds covering their bodies and upon further investigation their son 8 year old Jacob was found also stabbed to death with his throat slit in his bed upstairs. Such a horrific scene was left behind that the police responding would be affected long after the investigation. It didn't take police long to realize that family photos around the home depicted a family of 4 instead of 3. The 12 year old daughter Jasmine was missing. Immediately police were concerned that they had a kidnapping on their hands. The sweet angelic looking daughter in the photos must have been victimized by the monster that did this to her family as well. However, the sweet loving family photos that the police encountered depicting a 12 year old girl were not the reality where Jasmine was concerned. Jasmine had started acting and dressing differently. She had new friends, she was getting in trouble and going off to wild parties and she had a 23 year old boyfriend that her parents detested here being with. That boyfriend was into drugs, drinking, and dark things like werewolves, vampires, and the Goth culture. In fact that boyfriend even claimed to be a werewolf himself and reportedly professed to liking the taste of blood. Jasmine Richardson was not missing because she had been kidnapped rather she was missing because she was responsible. It would be later discovered that Jasmine and her 23 year old boyfriend, Jeremy Steinke had committed the murders themselves and had gone on the run.

Background

Once upon a time Jasmine Richardson was the sweet little girl depicted in the family photos around the Richardson house. Once upon a time the family was the perfect poster family for suburban bliss but something went wrong. Jasmine became interested in the Goth culture as well as the Wiccan religion. With this interest came a dark side to the little girl.

At 12 the little girl looked much older; perhaps 15 or 16 and she even claimed to be that old on social media. Soon she had the attention of local man Jeremy Steinke. Jasmine and Jeremy fell into a dangerous relationship. They idolized a life of negativity. They dressed in dark fantasy type clothing and they frequented sites on the internet like vampire freaks, a social media site for teens that love all things vampire. In fact Jeremy himself claimed to love the taste of blood and that he was a 300 year old werewolf. Jeremy had more practice at the twisted lifestyle that they both began to lead than Jasmine did but he was also weakened by a controlling effect that Jasmine had on him. Jasmine knew how to manipulate Jeremy. In many ways this seemed to spell love for Jeremy; he had found a girl that he would do anything for. In Jasmine's case Jeremy was an adult that she could control. She might have to live under what felt like the tyranny of her parents and she might have to go by the rules at the strict Catholic school that she attended but with Jeremy she had the say so. She could only wish for something and Jeremy was there to try to make her wishes come true. This might all sound like the musings of a warped but innocent mind, a reality created by dissatisfied kids looking to feel like they have more control over their lives but Jasmine and Jeremy took things much farther than most kids would dare to go. Just like any good loving parents the Richardsons became alarmed when they learned of the changes in their daughter's lifestyle. The most alarming thing to Jasmine's parents was Jeremy. No parent is going to be comfortable with their 12 year old little girl being in a relationship with a 23 year old man. More alarmingly their relationship was sexual as well. Jasmine may have looked much older but she still had the mind and body of a 12 year old girl chronologically speaking.

When Jasmine told Jeremy online that she had a plan to kill her family he hopped on board. They wrote instant messages to each other discussing the killing of Jasmine's family. Below are the exact words they typed to each other in a snippet of their conversation.

Jasmine: "I have this plan. It begins with me killing them and ends with me living with you."

Jeremy: "I love your plan but we need to get a little more creative with like details and stuff."

Who knows now if either of them were truly serious about committing the murders in the beginning but in the end Jeremy got pumped up watching the movie *Natural Born Killers,* got drunk, did some lines of cocaine and then he was ready to help his beloved carry out her request to alleviate herself of her bothersome parents. All it took was a set of loving protective parents trying to protect their 12 year old daughter from the psychological and perhaps even physical damage that would come from having a sexual relationship with a 23 year old man and Jasmine and Jeremy were all too ready to put an end to the two nuisances trying to keep them apart.

On the night of April 22nd Jeremy watched *Natural Born Killers* with his friends, did some drinking and drugs and then he was ready. He would do anything to make Jasmine happy. Despite her young age and the considerable age gap between the two Jasmine knew how to manipulate Jeremy. Jeremy snuck into the basement of The

Richardson's split level home and waited. Thinking she heard noises Debra Richardson, already in her night gown, went down to investigate. She couldn't have been prepared for what awaited her. As soon as Debra flipped on the light switch Jeremy attacked her stabbing her 12 times before killing her. Debra's husband Marc was close behind after hearing the commotion and armed with a screwdriver. However, in the end his screwdriver was no match for Jeremy's knife. Later Jeremy would tell an undercover police officer that he was worried Marc would get the better of him and that Marc nearly succeeded in defending himself with that screwdriver. No matter the fight Marc put up the scene ended up with him on the floor still in a defensive stance, dead with 24 stab wounds. Later Jeremy would say that Marc asked 'why' just before he died and Jeremy replied, 'it's what your daughter wanted.'

After killing Marc and Debra Jeremy headed upstairs leaving a trail of blood in his wake. Upstairs Jasmine was trying to calm her little brother down. At this point Jeremy and Jasmine's stories are not the same. Both of them say it was the other that actually killed the little boy. I suppose we will never know the truth nevertheless young Jacob was found in his bed with stab wounds in his body and his throat slit side to side. Jasmine and Jeremy left the scene and reportedly went back to a friend's apartment to have sex after obliterating Jasmine's entire family. They were the outlaw lovers that they had dreamed of being bound together even more so by the horrific blood bath they had just caused. The two went on the run but they didn't make it far. After a search of Jasmine's school locker a graphic picture surfaced of a girl's whole family burning in a fire while she laughs and escapes with her boyfriend. When police saw this drawing they went from searching for Jasmine as a victim to searching for her as a suspect.

Jasmine and Jeremy were apprehended in Saskatchewan the very next day after the bodies of her family were discovered. The pair were reportedly laughing and joking around with friends about the murders only one day after they had taken place.

Unfathomable Murder

The Richardsons were the picturesque family living in a picturesque neighborhood. Ross Glen, the community where the Richardsons lived, was a middle class neighborhood full of working class families. Their neighbors on one side were Sara and her six year old son Gareth, Jacob's best friend, and their neighbors on the other side were Phyllis and Vernon Gehring. The Gehrings were an elderly couple that liked to garden and look after their dog, a shi tzu Bishon mix. Often the scene would be that Gareth and Jacob could be found playing in the backyard as children do and the Gehrings would delight in tossing balls back over the fence when they strayed a bit too far. The Gehrings felt like Jacob kept them young. They admittedly didn't know much about the daughter. Just the night before that fateful afternoon when the bodies were found Marc Richardson had grilled hot dogs in the backyard for the boys while the Gehring's dog played with the Richardson family's dog through the fence. Everything seemed perfect in that sleepy little neighborhood until that fateful afternoon on April 23rd when Gareth went looking for his best friend.

It was about 1pm and Sara and Gareth had been at Sara's mom's house but Gareth had been asking to play with Jacob all morning. When Gareth could not get anyone to answer the phone at the Richardson residence Sara told him that they could go to the movies. Gareth was still bummed out about not getting to see Jacob and when he and his mom returned home before heading to the movies he darted over to the Richardson's after seeing that Marc's white pickup truck was in the driveway. Gareth knocked on the door but there was no answer, as a curious little boy might he began peering into the basement windows of the split level home. When he saw lifeless bodies and a basement covered in blood he ran back to his mom to tell her what he'd seen. Although Gareth wasn't usually the type of boy to make up stories the things he was saying to Sara just didn't make sense. As she followed him over to the neighbor's house she warned him that he had better not be lying. Sadly Gareth was not lying. When she peered through the same windows that Gareth had Sara saw a horrible scene in front of her. She was afraid that the intruder that had done this was still around, maybe he was even in her house waiting for her and Gareth. She called her mom and her mom told her she had to call 911. Sara's mom and the police headed to the scene. What would unfold at that crime scene would haunt police officers that investigated for years to come. Some of the officers involved were touched so much by young Jacob's defiled body that they broke down on the stand months later when they had to talk about it.

The police came in thinking that they might have an intruder still lurking about the property. They entered with caution. What they saw was unfathomable. There were the bodies of a man and woman in the basement both covered in blood. The woman, Debra Richardson was slumped in the floor with her night gown hiked up exposing the fact that all she had been wearing when she was attacked was that night gown. There was blood all over her and a pool of blood all around her. The little black family dog was standing beside her. Perhaps he felt that he needed to protect her but sadly it was too late for that. Across the basement slumped against a wall was Marc Richardson. His hands were straight out as though he were trying to defend himself. He was frozen by rigor mortis in a defensive state that did nothing for his defense in the end. Marc was wearing only black boxer shorts and a screwdriver was lying beside him. He, too, was riddled with stab wounds. The entire basement was covered in splatters of blood, there had been a real struggle between the Richardsons and their assailant. Upon further investigation of the house the police came across their worst nightmare. The first bedroom was empty but the next bedroom they came to was Jacob's. Jacob was lying in his bed. Police had hope for a moment that the boy was still alive but when they approached they were greeted with the worst. Jacob was in his bed with his throat slashed and stab wounds littering his body as well. There was blood all over his room including many of his toys. A toy light saber was lying in his floor; a useless object against the onslaught of the knife that had ended his life. In the master bedroom the comforter was thrown back as though the bed's occupants had left in a hurry. There was a pillow thrown awkwardly in the floor. Police wondered with horror if the boy had heard his parents being attacked before the assailant ever made it upstairs to him and clutched the pillow trying to find some comfort in the act. As they made another sweep of the house the police noticed that there were four members of the Richardson family instead of three. Instantly everyone's heart sank. A family photo depicted a sweet smiling 12 year old girl and she was nowhere to be found. Police searched that house several times over for either the body of the little girl or perhaps the girl hiding somewhere too afraid to come out after the horrible things she had witnessed but in the end they had to admit defeat, the fourth member of the Richardson family was nowhere to be seen. On the plus side her body wasn't there slain with the rest of her family but the police had to think the worst. The most logical thought was that she may have been kidnapped by whoever did this to her family. And even if she was safe, perhaps spending the night at a friend's house she would still have to deal with the tragic news that she had no family left, that her family had all been brutally attacked and killed. Hearts went out for the girl and for the family she had lost. No one wanted to be left breaking that news to a 12 year old.

The hunt for Jasmine Richardson began, or actually continued, as her parents had reported that she was missing before the terrible crime had ever even taken place. Where was Jasmine? Safe, but oblivious to the fact that this terrible thing had happened to her parents? Scared alone and possibly seriously injured in the hands of the monster that did this to her family? No one could say. As part of the investigation police visited Jasmine's school and got permission to look inside her locker. They were looking for any kind of evidence that would lead them to Jasmine whatsoever but what they found was truly a shocking discovery. When the police searched Jasmine's locker they found a hand drawn picture depicting a horrible scene. In the picture a girl's family burns to death after she puts gasoline in the sprinklers while they have a family picnic. The stick figure girl in the drawing laughs as her family burns and she escapes in her boyfriend's pickup truck. This drawing shifted suspicions entirely and Jasmine Richardson went from being searched for as a victim to being searched for as a suspect in the murder of her parents and her little brother. Consequently it didn't take the police long to track Jasmine and Jeremy down. The pair were said to be joking around with friends about the murders even at the time of apprehension. They were found at a high school in Saskatchewan only about 60 miles from Medicine Hat.

Both Jasmine and Jeremy were jailed and both were convicted. Because of Jasmine's young age at the time under Canadian law she had to be referred to as JR instead of her name. She also was protected from being tried as an adult. Although she got the maximum sentence for a child her age that sentence was only 10 years and under the conditions the time she had already spent in jail counted toward her 10 years. She ended up being imprisoned under the conditions of 4 years locked up undergoing rehabilitation and 4.5 years under very close supervision in the community. Jeremy, on the other hand, was 23 years old at the time of the murders. He was found guilty of three counts of first degree murder and sentenced to three life sentences to be served consecutively. An undercover officer rode with Jeremy while he was being transported from one facility to the other. In the conversation the two had together Jeremy expressed that he loved Jasmine more than anything and that the kind of thing he did was the kind of thing that truly expressed that love. He admitted to everything he did in such a straight forward way that it seemed he did not even grasp the gravity of the situation. He even shared his plans to marry Jasmine when they were both able to get out of prison. On murderpedia.org you can actually read the transcript of the conversation that Jeremy had with the undercover officer that he believed to be another prison being transported along with him. Steinke will be eligible for parole after 25 years.

Some of the residents of Medicine Hat were actually outraged with the outcome of the trial. They didn't think that justice would be served with Jasmine getting away with such little time. Wayne Chopek is one such resident that has spoken out about his outrage. Wayne was a friend of the family and he is disgusted at the fact that Jasmine would go free after a short ten years. However, the law remains the law and in Canada the government believes that children as young as Jasmine was at the time of the murders need to be rehabilitated rather than being locked up and having the key thrown away. They believe that such young lives have more potential value than to doom them to the rest of their lives behind bars.

Life After Murder

After Jasmine and Jeremy were arrested and jailed they still held onto the flame that was recklessly burning before the murders. They were not able to have any contact with one another except for letter writing so they wrote back and forth. This is how Jeremy came to ask Jasmine to marry him and she said yes. Below is an excerpt of the letters passed between the two when Jeremy popped the question.

Jeremy: "Without you this life isn't worth living... U said you want to get engaged? Then here's a Q...Will U marry me? If so then it is a verbal agreement!"

Jasmine: "Ahahaha! I never thought I'd find myself hystericaly laughing in a holding cell in these kinds of circumstances...or ever really. But still! ahaha you make me so happy! Yes! Yes! I will, I would love to... "

Interestingly enough as bright as that flame might have been it eventually flickered out. Although they professed the deepest of bonds neither of the two would admit to actually being the one to Kill Jacob. Both blamed the other. This was one of the deciding factors that actually showed that there were holes in the loving couple's relationship. The two broke up in jail. After incarceration the relationship that had been important enough to kill for dwindled until it was no more.

Perhaps free of any attachment to Jeremy Steinke Jasmine could truly rehabilitate. Jasmine underwent psychiatric evaluations and was determined to be suffering from oppositional defiance disorder as well as conduct disorder. When she first started therapy she was determined to suffer from dependency issues, anxiety and depression. As well as all this she was prone to immature problem solving and wishful fantasies. All this is a lot to bog down a 12 year old but was it enough of a load to excuse the execution of the murder of her entire family? Many say no, some say yes. At any rate it is indeed enough to at least explain some of her behaviors. Once in therapy Jasmine began making progress toward rehabilitation though in the beginning her details of how things played out her a bit skewed to reality. By 2010 Jasmine was making significant progress in her rehabilitation and had professed to be sorry for the crimes she committed. As the terms of her sentencing were laid out she got credit on her sentence for the time she spent in jail awaiting trial and then after 4 years of incarceration she was deemed fit enough to go into the community under very close supervision for 4.5 years. During that time Jasmine was shown to exhibit exemplary behavior as well as being a straight A student. Jasmine was admitted to Calgary University where she continued to earn really high grades. This year, 2016, in May Jasmine became a completely free woman. The courts have no reason to think that she is a danger to society any longer. It's been a decade and she has been through extensive amounts of therapy and shown nothing but progress in that entire time.

A very interesting thing to look at here is the chemistry between Jasmine and Jeremy. One asks themselves, was the combination just toxic? Would either of them been capable of doing something like this on their own? It seems that the pairing of the two and the dependency that both of them exhibited for the other was actual such an explosive combination that it pushed them over the edge just enough to create the perfect circumstance for this to happen. Jasmine has said that she wasn't really being serious when she would send Jeremy messages saying that she had a plan to kill her parents and live with him. That she didn't really mean to go through with it when she joked about murdering her family or made drawings depicting their deaths. But she felt those feelings and she told Jeremy. Steinke just happened to be easily manipulated, a regular user of multiple drugs, and even believed himself to be a 300 year old werewolf. Jeremy and Jasmine both took the dark Goth culture they lived within to the extreme. They exchanged vials of blood and Jeremy wore one around his neck. When the two were faced with Jasmine's parents making them unable to see one another dark fantasies were transformed into evil realities. Perhaps the fantasies that both harbored were purely fantasies until the tension kept rising and rising and the two kept feeding off of each other until the combination of each of their dark thoughts breathed life into the other. In the end it doesn't really matter to ask if either would have been capable of the atrocity on their own because it wasn't the case that they were on their own. They were bound together by an obsessive unhealthy love and the obsessive unhealthy thoughts in both their heads took form in reality. The result was unspeakable horror.

That late April day three lives were lost much too soon and in such a violent way that it is nearly unthinkable. That alone is enough to make this tragedy stand out forever in history but that's not all that was lost. Little Gareth will never be the same. Though he is a successful high schooler now the memory of those bodies and the memory of the loss of his best friend will always be with him. And of course Jasmine Richardson and Jeremy Steinke's lives will forever be changed and affected. Jeremy will most likely spend his entire life in jail having had only 23 short years of freedom. Parole will be an unlikely event. Even though Jasmine has improved and rehabilitated, even if she successfully integrates back into society, she will forever have this as a part of her past. She will also forever have people that look at her as a monster. Her story is known all over the world. Jasmine is the youngest person in Canada to have ever committed such a heinous crime. It is a question to ponder as to whether Jasmine has forgiven herself or if she is forever haunted by the monster that she perhaps did not even know lurked inside her. Perhaps even scarier to think of is the possibility that she really could live without being constantly haunted by the crime. Is there any amount of rehabilitation that should erase that guilt? And then one has to consider Jeremy. Has he come to terms with the events? Is he sorry for his crimes? Will a life in prison in any way begin to repay his debt for those three lives that he so brutally extinguished?

Life in Medicine Hat continues on. It is still a relatively safe place to live. Medicine Hat is still a relatively small tight knit place filled with working class suburbs. There are still nice neighborhoods that feel safe the way that Ross Glen did before tragedy came to town but no one will forget what could happen no matter how nice or normal a family might seem they will know that a tragedy like this could happen to any family because it already has.

GIRL MONSTER : THE TRUE STORY OF BROOKEY LEE WEST

SARAH SANCHEZ

One of the most gruesome and bizarre crimes that ever occurred in Las Vegas was discovered on February 5, 2001. The manager of Canyon Gate Mini Storage, Bill Unruh, opened Unit #317 after someone reported a very bad smell.

He found a 45-gallon garbage container that had a brownish liquid oozing out of it at the bottom. He called police.

Detectives entered a unit that contained normal items on one side and the oozing sealed-up garbage container on the other side. There were also books about witchcraft and Satanism in the locker.

Unruh told police that the unit had been rented in the names of Brookey Lee West and Christine Smith on June 26, 1998.

The garbage container had been made airtight with duct tape, packing tape, plastic wrap, and garbage bags. The leakage was coming from a hole that had developed in the bottom.

When investigators cut the container open, more fluid seeped out accompanied by dead maggots. They could see a human body inside, very decomposed. The body was mostly liquefied, but those on scene could easily see that a white plastic bag was tied around the person's face.

Crime scene analysts tested the brownish liquid for human blood and the test was positive.

In the storage unit, Detective David Mesinar found Christine Smith's wallet, ID, prescriptions, and documents relating to her Social Security payments.

Dental records confirmed that the body was Christine's. Christine would have been 68 years old if she was still alive.

Detectives began by looking for Christine's daughter, 46-year-old Brookey Lee West.

Brookey is now serving life without parole for murdering her mother. Brookey may also have murdered her brother Travis and probably murdered her third husband Howard.

Brookey's mother Christine, her father Leroy, her husband Howard, Brookey herself, and Brookey's brother Travis all had tragic childhoods and went on to live destructive or self-destructive lives.

On hearing this story, some might be amazed that nobody killed Christine before she reached her 60s. By all accounts, she was a sociopathic parasite who had never worked a day in her life other than her short degrading stint as a prostitute at the age of sixteen.

By the time her daughter killed her, though, she was a harmless pain in the ass with major health problems and suffering from dementia.

Christine's Childhood

Christine Merle Sands was born on February 14, 1932, in Ennis, Ellis County, Texas. Her parents were Clyde and Annie Sands. As it was for many people during the Great Depression, life was a struggle.

Ennis was a hub for the cotton industry, and Clyde worked as a long haul trucker moving cotton products. He also worked as a lineman installing power lines across the country. The lineman job was very demanding physically, but it paid well when the work was available. Even with both jobs, money was always tight.

Clyde's work often took him away from home for long periods leaving Annie to run the home.

Annie was a housewife and a loving woman. The Sands were not abusive parents, but day-to-day life didn't allow them the time or capacity to nurture their six children.

Trudy was born in 1911. She was followed by Woodrow, Lawrence, Richard Bob, Billy, and finally Christine in 1932.

The two youngest children, Billy and Christine, made it to the eighth grade before they dropped out of school. Their parents had no concept of the importance of education, so this was not an issue in the family.

Christine later told Brookey that a family member had begun molesting her at the age of eight. Billy knows nothing about this, but such a thing would not have been talked about within a family in 1930s Texas.

Billy does say that Christine was a good girl who started to spin out of control around the age of ten.

When she dropped out of school, Christine was thirteen years old. By sixteen, she had gone off the rails. Says Billy, "I think, personally, she was restless at home by herself . . . she was looking for anything that come along so she could grab a hold of it and get out of little old Ennis."

At sixteen, Christine married a young man. This is how Billy describes him: "He was a bad character. I don't know what in the world she ever seen in him, because he was really something . . . It was bad from the word go. Several people said he treated her like a dog."

Christine and her new husband ran off to Houston. According to Billy's wife JoAnn, the husband was very abusive. Very soon, he had turned her out as a Houston whore. Christine felt degraded and she was very angry. She got her daddy to come and take her back to Ennis.

Leroy's Childhood

Leroy was born in Russia. When he was a baby, his family moved to the U.S. and settled in the hills of Tennessee.

His parents' marriage was violent. His father murdered his mother during a domestic dispute. According to West, "He cut her head off with a machete in Tennessee . . . my dad said his father went to prison for about ten years." Leroy was five at the time.

Leroy's older sisters pinned a note to his jacket explaining that he was an orphan and put him on a bus. He ended up alone on a city street corner. The woman who found him gave him to another woman, an alcoholic who was unable to have children. She and her husband thought that being childless made them look bad so they took him in.

His new parents, named Smith, took him to Arkansas and named him Leroy.

Leroy told his own family later that much of his time as a member of the Smith family was spent living in tents and shacks.

At sixteen, determined to get away from that family, he lied about his age and enlisted in the army. His love of guns began in the army. He also liked the military discipline and the structure it imposed.

By then he was already defensive, antisocial, reclusive, filled with anger, and very racist.

West said about her father, "My dad didn't like nothing that wasn't white. That's just the way he was. I used to tell him, 'You know what, Dad? If you tried to join the skinheads, you would be president of them in six months.' He would be like, 'Yeah, I would be.'"

Leroy & Christine

Leroy Smith was stationed at Fort Bliss in El Paso, Texas, when he met Christine Sands in 1947. It's not clear what she was doing in El Paso, 600 miles from Ennis.

She was sixteen, freshly out of her disastrous first marriage. She had blue eyes, long blond hair, and a sexy figure in a tight dress. He was eighteen and looked very fine in his army uniform. They had a lust-hate relationship from the start. They were both infatuated, but his arrogance ticked her off. Her attitude ticked him off but it also made him want her.

They dated on his weekends off. It was casual for him, but she was not going to let this handsome army guy out of her grasp. Soon Christine was "pregnant."

According to Brookey, "My dad said that's why he married her. He told me he wanted to divorce her after he was married to her for about three months. He said, 'I knew I'd been had.'"

Leroy As A Cop – Leroy Gets Into Drugs

Shortly after the marriage, Leroy left the army and was hired as a patrol officer with the El Paso Police Department. El Paso was crawling with drug dealers, drug smugglers, pimps, and prostitutes in the early 1950s. Whatever his motives may have been when he signed up, Leroy soon dove into the muck.

"This is when my father started using drugs, and this is also about the time my mom started using drugs, too," Brookey says.

Leroy told West that he made extra money by shaking down drug dealers. "He'd take dope from some suspect and give it to some snitch to sell it to somebody."

Leroy's drug of preference was speed. He started taking it because he needed energy when he was on night shift, but soon he was popping pills every day. Being a crooked cop in a city full of Mexican-American criminals was right up Leroy's racist alley.

According to Brookey, "It was getting to the point where he was getting really violent. My dad wouldn't back down from anybody, and he had a real bad temper."

At this time, Christine was also doing drugs and beginning to behave strangely. She began to lie all the time and for no reason. One of her favorite lies was that she was Cherokee. Sometimes she was Apache. According to Chloe Smith, Leroy's second wife, this drove Leroy crazy as he thought of Native Americans as "savages."

The couple's life was out of control before they were even twenty years old, before their children were born.

Leroy cheated on Christine constantly. As a cop, he had a lot of access. Leroy later told Chloe Smith that he didn't even try to hide it from Christine because she wasn't interested in sex anyway. He also thought Christine was crazy.

While Leroy was at work, shaking down drug dealers and getting it on with prostitutes, Christine was either in the bars downtown or sitting in the apartment smoking, drinking, and popping pills.

They were fighting constantly and violently by 1951. One time, Christine, in a drunken stupor, crawled into bed, put a gun to Leroy's head, and pulled the trigger. There were no bullets in the gun so she put it under her pillow and went to sleep. Leroy later told Brookey that he had awakened when Christine entered the room and, knowing the gun was empty, pretended to be still asleep.

Brookey Lee West: "Who knows why? But my mother didn't really need a reason to kill anybody. My mother was a very devious person."

Leroy & Christine Pregnant

In 1952, Leroy decided to leave and move on with his life. That's when Christine announced that she was pregnant.

Leroy later told his second wife, "She never got pregnant, she never got pregnant, never got pregnant. Then, when the pressure was on, suddenly it happened."

Eventually it was obvious that she was telling the truth about being pregnant, but Leroy always wondered if Brookey was really his child.

Brookey Is Born

Brookey Lee Smith was born in an El Paso hospital on June 28, 1953. Both parents fell in love with her sweet nature, brown hair, and hazel eyes. As a toddler, she loved her parents and all she cared about was pleasing them.

When Christine took time off from partying, she took Brookey to Aunt Trudy's house or to the park to play. But both of her parents were drug addicts and alcoholics, so Brookey was often left home alone.

Travis Is Born

In 1956, Christine was pregnant again.

West says, "My dad was furious with her . . . 'You just did this to put another rope around my neck!' I heard that for years."

Travis Lee Smith was born August 29, 1956. West recollects, "My brother was a chubby, heavy baby. They put these striped shirts on him, and he looked like a wrestler."

Unlike Brookey, Travis was a problem child from the start. West thinks he may have had ADHD: "He would chew on Sheetrock . . . he was something else. He was like my mother in that he did not have a good disposition. Him and my mother adored each other."

Little Travis was born with a tongue that was too long for his mouth. This made it difficult for him to nurse from a bottle and he had a speech impediment most of his life. People thought he was slow, but he wasn't. They couldn't understand the language he had made up for himself.

Travis was a biter as a tot, and his mother encouraged him to bite people and children. The other kids called him "the snapping turtle."

Brookey & Travis' Early Life

Family snapshots show that the early lives of Brookey and Travis were not total hell. Their smiles in the pictures show that they had some fun times with their parents. But most of the time they were lonely and abandoned.

Brookey made paper dolls and dressed them up as fantasy queens or princesses. She recalls that she only had one birthday party, because her parents were too busy partying to put it together most years. She looked after Travis for days at a time while her parents were out barhopping.

West says, "We had all kinds of medications in our cabinets. Speed, then tranquilizers to calm [them] down." Her mother told her years later that they were both too strung out to be decent parents.

Leroy Is Fired & The Smiths Move To California

In the mid-1950s, Leroy was fired from the police department. He told Brookey and others that it was because he had borrowed money from the police department – which was apparently a normal thing – but didn't return it as per SOP.

Chloe, Leroy's second wife, thinks that it was something worse than that. Leaving the El Paso PD was a sore topic with him when he met her more than twenty years later. Considering his activities as a cop – shaking down drug dealers, getting snitches to sell drugs for him, and using prostitutes as his personal harem – Chloe may well be right.

In 1959, the Smiths headed west. They stayed in cheap motels in New Mexico and Ventura, California, before they chose to settle in Bakersfield, California.

Bakersfield was an oil city full of Texans and Oklahomans who had migrated there during the Depression. It was a honky-tonk town and Leroy and Christine totally belonged.

Leroy found a steady job putting down carpet in houses and was able to rent a home in a low-income neighborhood.

Brookey describes the neighborhood: "Most of them are just like my parents. Alcoholics, drinkers, partiers, sitting out in front of their homes drinking and working on some old wrecked-out car, saying, 'Go in the house there, baby, and get daddy a beer! Go in there and get me my shotgun!' They'd all be out there shouting at each other in the yard with their rifles pointed at each other."

Leroy and Christine partied hard in the Bakersfield bar scene. Brookey, seven, had to look after Travis, four. Sometimes for two to three days at a stretch.

During work hours, Leroy laid carpet while Christine spent all day in bed recovering. She always had aches and pains. But when Leroy came home and wanted to go out, Christine was ready to party.

How Leroy managed to spend his days laying carpet is hard to guess. He popped amphetamines and tranquilizers, and he drank wine all the time. He didn't seem to care about what booze and drugs might be doing to him.

The Smith Family Goes Downhill In Bakersfield

West described the next step in her parents' spiral: "That's about the time when my parents started going to doctors to get more and more pills. They were writing prescriptions for my parents for painkillers, and then my parents would sell them. Sell them to their friends or whoever wanted them . . . that's how they made their money."

She added, "I took care of them and all their problems. If I could hide something for them, I did. If they told me to lie, I lied. Someone would call up and say, 'Can I speak to your dad?' And I'd say, 'Well, he's not here. He went to a doctor.' Meanwhile, my dad was right there smashed out of his mind."

Around this time, Leroy's drunken rages sometimes became so violent that his spankings left bruises on their bottoms in the shape of his hand. According to West. "There were times that he would spank us with a two-by-four. I'd go to school with bruises all over, but no one ever said anything."

The house was full of guns. They were even underneath the beds and the cushions of the couch. Leroy also carried a gun.

He once threatened to kill a man who was driving too fast in their neighborhood.

He told the guy after pulling him out of his car, "You see all these kids around here? If you want to run over somebody's kid, make sure you run over somebody else's, because if you run over one of my kids, I'm going to twist your head off your shoulders and use it as a doorknob."

Christine was a screamer rather than a hitter. Brookey was afraid of both of them and learned to be careful. Brookey and Travis were treated the way their parents had been treated as children. As objects.

The alcohol, drugs, neglect, arguments, and violence damaged both children emotionally.

Added to that stress on the children, their parents kept splitting up and getting back together. There was constant talk of divorce. Christine would disappear for days and then

Leroy would disappear for days. The children couldn't help thinking that everything was their fault.

Leroy & Christine Break Up – Christine Shoots Her Lover & Goes To Prison

In 1961, Leroy left Christine for a waitress named Faye. He moved Brookey and Travis into Faye's house with Faye's six kids.

Meanwhile, Christine hooked up with a married man. He worked as a mason. They had a steamy romance for a few months. He promised her they would have a new life together somewhere.

According to Christine, they had been planning to kill his wife with "sleeping medicine, a lot of sleeping stuff."

Christine told police in a taped admission: "He wanted me to kill her, and I thought, 'You son of a bitch, if I killed her, where would I be with you?' Who would he get to kill me? That's the way I felt about it."

In the early weeks of 1961, the man told Christine he was going back to his wife. She was angry. She told police later, "I said, 'Well, you know, you can take me to the water, you son of a bitch, but ain't going to drown me because I'll kill your ass.'"

On January 24, 1961, Christine asked the man and his wife to meet her at a bar in Bakersfield to help her plan how to get her own marriage back on track. She showed up at 7:30 p.m. as arranged. She had a sawed-off 16-guage shotgun on her lap, hidden by her jacket and sweater.

The couple showed up a few minutes later and sat down. Christine reached under the table, pulled the trigger, and shot him.

The man, aged thirty, was rushed to a hospital with blood pouring out of him. His arm had been shattered, but his life was saved through surgery.

Christine, aged twenty-eight, was taken away in handcuffs. She later told police, "I didn't have the least feeling of sympathy. Hell, no." In fact, she bragged about it for the rest of her life. She also told police at the time that she did not know where Brookey and Travis were living.

Life During Christine's Trial

Leroy's relationship with Faye was falling apart. He took Brookey and Travis back to live in Christine's home while they waited for Christine's day in court.

Brookey found this time very traumatic. She was only eight, and her mother's crime was on the television news. She was very ashamed of her mother.

West remembers going with her father to visit her mother in jail and at the trial: "My dad took a dress down to her, and it was a honky-tonk dress with no back, so her lawyers put a sweater around her because they didn't want her in court in that thing. They wrote in the paper that she was a Lolita."

In March 1961, Christine was sent to the California Institute for Women (CIA) with a sentence of fourteen years for assault with intent to commit murder.

Brookey later said, "My mother talked about that shooting like she was some sort of movie star. The first thing out of her mouth about it was, 'Well, you know, I went to prison because I shot that son of a bitch. He deserved it.'"

Christine In Prison

Christine fit in well with the people in prison. She had always been a manipulative person and knew how to connect with people. She worked it there too. As a kitchen worker, she sneaked extra sweets to certain inmates. Some were outraged when she was moved out of kitchen duty to another job.

Brookey & Travis After Christine Is Sent To Prison

Brookey, aged eight, didn't fare well after all of this. She couldn't pay attention in school. She didn't talk about her situation to friends or teachers. She failed second grade.

Travis, aged five, was completely traumatized. Leroy told Brookey to be an adult and tell Travis that his mother was dead and buried. If she was to be treated as an adult, she should act like one. She did what she was told.

Within a year of Christine being in prison, Leroy and the kids lived in Fresno, then Oregon, then San Luis Obispo, and ended up back in Bakersfield.

As Brookey describes it, they were always worried, they were always moving, there was always trauma. She says of her dad, "Drink all day and half the night. It was getting to where he couldn't even work anymore. We were living in another run-down motel, and he was feeding us crackers for dinner. Pillar to post and motel to motel. If you didn't have something to eat that day, you asked the neighbors for something."

Orphanage

In 1962, Leroy decided that the children would be better off without him. His drinking was more important than looking after them, maybe. They had not heard from their mother since she'd gone to prison.

He dropped them off at the Sunnycrest Home for Youths in Bakersfield. Brookey was screaming that she would be good if he let them come home.

As it turned out, Brookey and Travis loved the orphanage. They went to school regularly, they got good grades, they were properly fed, and they had clothes to wear. The place was run by a loving older couple.

Travis, in particular, became attached to the couple. Brookey did not miss her parents. Both of them would have loved to stay there forever.

Christine Gets Out Of Jail, The Smiths Move To San Jose

One day, Leroy showed up at the orphanage with Christine in the car. She had been paroled after serving only two years of her sentence. She had five years of probation to go yet. Travis cried and screamed – he did not want to leave the orphanage. But leave he did.

Brookey Lee West's take on this is that her parents "sought each other out after my mom got out of prison because it was one of those types of relationships, like when an abused woman keeps going back to her husband. They didn't want each other, but then, when they were apart, they really did. And then, they didn't want each other again. That's the way their relationship was. On and off all the time."

San Jose

In 1965, the family moved to San Jose, now known as Silicone Valley. Any stability the children had enjoyed at the orphanage was gone forever now. Christine was back in their lives and San Jose was where Leroy would dedicate himself to Satan.

Leroy got another job laying carpet and rented a house on Lafayette Street, a mostly Hispanic neighborhood.

Brookey, as a white kid, didn't fit in. She played alone or with her brother.

She says, "The kids weren't very friendly to me. I was always big for my age, and by the time I was twelve, I was tall. I didn't look twelve, and I didn't look like everyone else."

Travis, only nine, was self-destructive and he was fighting. "My brother started using drugs when he was nine," Brookey says. "Pills right out of the cabinet. The bathroom cabinet couldn't hold all these pills. Any color you wanted."

Leroy Embraces Satanism

The family had a friend who lived about six blocks away that West only knows as "Mrs. Beauford." Leroy was especially close to her.

One day, Brookey, aged thirteen, was sent there by her mother to return a borrowed dish. "I knocked on her door, the door sort of came open and I said hello, and nobody answered. I stood there for a second, and I hear this moaning, groaning, kind of like screaming. It's coming from the basement."

When she went to the back of the house, she saw a bunch of people doing a spell or something.

Leroy got into the spells and witchcraft quickly. The idea of making enemies suffer was enticing to him. By the late 1960s he was a regular participant in the ceremonies with all the candles, robes, and chants that anyone might imagine.

Of course, none of this was unusual in California in the 1960s and 1970s. But Leroy started to believe that he was a warlock with a high rank in Satan's legion.

West's take on this: "He had books, knives and other stuff. They wore their robes, almost like the Ku Klux Klan, and it was a secretive organization . . . My dad identified with that stuff. He didn't go around killing people, but he believed Satan was the ruler of this world, and he could give you anything you wanted. You just have to know how to get in touch."

West claims that she understands all of this, has read a lot about it, that it is valid, and that true believers can actually cast spells that work. She says she has not practiced it herself but knows of people in very high positions who do.

Brookey In High School

At the age of fourteen, Brookey was attending Santa Clara High School in Jan Jose. By this time she was very attractive. She had hazel eyes, curly brown hair, a shapely body, and gorgeous legs from doing ballet. She wore the same type of clothes her mom had worn in the Bakersfield honky-tonk days.

West: "I dressed very sexy. I was a looker. The boys all wanted a date with me, but I didn't want to go. I was very standoffish about men. Probably because of the way my home life was, I couldn't invite anybody home."

She had lower than average grades, she was aimless, and she had no plans.

Smith Family Late 1960s

In the late 1960s, Leroy wasn't trying to hide his affairs. He was also drinking very heavily. Christine was fed up and moved out. The resulting divorce was traumatic for Brookey and Travis.

Travis simply dropped out of school to do drugs. It was all he cared about ever again, really. He loved speed and meth. He didn't want to work, though Leroy tried to get him involved in the carpet laying job. He lied and stole to get drugs and was always in legal trouble.

Christine, after years of doing drugs and booze all day every day, joined Alcoholics Anonymous and was eventually successful at quitting both.

She joined a church and got Brookey to attend services with her. She wanted to understand all the traumas of her life, the molestation, being turned into a hooker by her first husband, why she married so young in the first place. Christine wanted to find God. Soon she was able to talk a good game about Jesus but, according to West, she wanted to be forgiven without putting in the work.

Christine was still full of spite and anger.

West explains: "My mom started going to church with me when I was in my teens, but she still viewed religion as a matter of convenience. She wasn't book smart enough to learn the Bible, or even read it, and she didn't apply herself."

Christine Is Actually Crazy

Christine had always experienced aches and pains, she always had a cough, she was always sick in bed. Even with her lifestyle – the smoking, drinking, and drugs – these problems were deemed psychosomatic and she was referred to a mental health clinic.

During her screening, she beat the doctor on the head with the heel of her boot. Authorities ordered her to see a state psychiatrist, Sydney Goldstein. She was a patient of his for the next ten years.

During one visit, Goldstein's receptionist told Brookey that Goldstein only took the sickest of patients. That's when Brookey first understood that Christine was seriously mentally ill.

She had an opportunity to snoop her mother's medical file, and in it she read that her mother was a "sociopath with psychopathic tendencies." Sociopaths care for nobody but themselves.

When discussing this eye-opener, West said, "She was a total sociopath."

Brookey Launches Out On Her Own

Brookey Lee Smith graduated from Santa Clara High School in 1971. It was time to get away from her insane mother, her Satanist warlock racist father, and her dropout druggy brother.

Her grades were lower than average, but she was accepted into the army. The army was not what she had imagined it to be. All the rules and restrictions seemed stupid to her. After nine months, she managed to get out honorably. She had wanted to be a spy.

She was broke and had no post-secondary education. At twenty years old, she was living with Christine, paying all the bills by working odd jobs, waitress jobs, legal secretary jobs. Christine had no job and Brookey desperately wanted to get away from her.

1973 – Brookey Has A Daughter

In 1973, Brookey met a man at the church she and her mother had been attending. Soon they were dating. He was handsome and smooth-talking. She considered him the love of her life.

Ronald Ray Veramontes "was good-looking, he was charming, so we dated for a while," says West. "We dated maybe six or seven months, and I was wild about him. I was in love with him. Completely gone."

Veramontes later told police that their relationship had never been serious.

Brookey got pregnant during a weekend trip to Los Angeles. "I just told him I was pregnant, straight up, and it was over the phone, because he called me to see how I was feeling. That's when he gave me this snotty-assed remark, saying, 'How do you know it's mine?' I'm naïve up to this point. I think I knew in my heart he was already out seeing other women on the side, but I really couldn't face that. As soon as I told him I was pregnant, he was gone," she said.

Brookey's parents were furious. "They called me all kinds of names. Bitch, whore, slut, a tramp. 'Why don't you have an abortion?'"

In 1974, at O'Connor Catholic Hospital, Brookey gave birth to a beautiful girl.

1977 – First Marriage Fizzles

Around 1977, Brookey saw a classified ad looking for a female singer for a country band. She was twenty-four and it sounded like a way to make some extra cash. The ad had been placed by a fifty-eight-year-old concert promoter who was an Okie to boot. He was infatuated with her and they were married within a few months.

"He was real good to me at first," she says. "The one thing I always thought was real good about him was he never tried to hit me, never tried to raise his hand toward me, even though we had some nasty arguments. That's the good things I can say about him. But he had drinking issues, dope issues, same thing all my husbands had. I guess it was the caretaker syndrome."

She sang in the band for a while. "You have to be drunk to sing that stuff," she said later.

She wasn't into singing in the band. After about six weeks, she said to him, "Who the hell are you? What do I want with you? This is just not working." They divorced.

1981 – Career In Silicon Valley Takes Off, Second Marriage Fizzles

Brookey eventually got a decent job as a security guard at National Advanced Systems, a computer company located in Palo Alto. Soon she became a secretary there, a much better job, and that is how she met her second husband "West."

She took some papers to his office. He asked her out. They became engaged during their first date and were married within five months. Brookey was twenty-eight and he was forty-nine.

According to Brookey's description, "He was tall, slender, very Norwegian, with sharp features. Good-looking, blond haired."

Christine didn't approve of Brookey marrying a man so much older. Mr. West though Christine was crazy and mean. They couldn't stand each other. They constantly fought. This marriage was also over within months.

Brookey blames her bipolar disorder for both of those marriages. She wasn't stable then, she says. She has a hatred for West that she doesn't have for her first husband.

She says that West molested her daughter during a school vacation. "If I would have had a reason to kill somebody, it would have probably been him. If I wanted to kill him for money, it would have been ideal, because he had $250,000 in life insurance," she says.

Before the divorce, she was set to inherit his estate if he died. "He signed everything over to me in case of his death, so if I had a reason to kill somebody, it would have been him."

Brookey Wants To Give Her Daughter Away

Brookey was working long hours as a legal secretary to support her mother and daughter. When the child was four, Brookey sent her to a boarding school in Arizona so she would not have to be left alone with crazy Christine. There weren't a lot of visits back and forth.

By the time her daughter was nine, around 1983, Brookey decided she wanted her daughter to stay with the people who ran the school. Brookey had mood swings. She was unstable. She did not think she could be a good parent.

But her daughter's father, Ray Veramontes, refused to give up his parental rights. He wanted to adopt her rather than let her be given away.

West was furious with him and so was Leroy. No Mexican was going to tell his daughter what to do.

According to Veramontes, "I wanted to have custody of my daughter, full custody. It was not up for conversation with them. It wasn't in their heads."

Veramontes Receives Witchy Threats

On January 14, 1985, a man dressed in black showed up at Veramontes' grandmother's house asking for "Ray." One witness said the man was wearing a Halloween mask. He shot her in the chest with a .22. With surgery, she survived.

On February 13, Veramontes received a handwritten letter with a pentagram drawn on it and satanic chants threatening the murder of his entire family. "You pray to your God, I'll pray to mine. We'll see whose God is stronger," it said.

He knew that Leroy was a warlock or a witch. Veramontes was terrified of what Leroy might do and gave up his custody battle. His daughter was adopted by the teachers in Arizona.

Brookey's Tech Writing Career

While working at National Advanced Systems, Brookey was promoted from her secretary position to working with hardware and mainframes. She was also studying everything she could find about programming, engineering, and troubleshooting. She was drawn to technical writing and turned out to be extremely good at it.

By the late 1980s and early 1990s, she was doing technical writing on contract for the best companies in Silicon Valley – including Sun, Intel, and Cisco – earning $65-$100 per hour.

She bought a house in Los Banos, wore expensive clothes, and drove a Jaguar.

But she still had Christine around her neck.

Brookey's Life With Christine

Christine was living with Brookey and living off Brookey. They lived together in a rental house in San Jose in the early 1990s before Brookey bought the house in Los Banos. Brookey was kept on her toes just trying to make sure her mother didn't do anything crazy.

Christine tried to poison a neighbor's dog with cayenne pepper and then with gopher poison. When Brookey asked her about it, Christine said, "Yeah, I did. I hate that son of a bitch." The dog survived.

Though they were always fighting, they also loved each other. Brookey had absorbed Christine's obsession with Native American culture. Now they were both claiming Native American roots, and they loved shopping for Indian jewelry and art.

Leroy Post-Christine: Chloe

Leroy's second wife, Chloe, had been through two failed marriages by 1975. She had two children from her first marriage. They were living with their father. She met Leroy while she was working at a tavern near Santa Clara University.

Chloe was born in Massachusetts. Her alcoholic father moved the family to rural Arizona in the 1940s. Their life was "pretty desolate and pretty awful."

Leroy was affectionate and protective. He made her feel special. They were married in 1977 and she hoped this marriage would be different.

They rented a house on Lawrence Street in San Jose. Leroy was still working as a carpet layer. Women still made him "sparkle and twinkle." He was still a hostile person who did not trust people. But he loved Chloe unconditionally and thrived on her stable nature. Chloe was so unlike Christine.

He came with a lot of baggage. He was always falling off the wagon. He was still a raging racist. He had guns hidden all over the house. During arguments, he would threaten to do to Chloe what his father had done to his mother.

During the twenty years they were married, Leroy explored a variety of religions. Chloe never saw Leroy engaged in any kind of devil worship, though in hindsight she can think of a couple of instances.

On one occasion, his Mexican neighbors had been parking in front of his house and he left them a satanic note similar to the one that Veramontes had received. He had an excuse for that – Mexicans are very religious and using religious stuff is a good way to get under their skin.

Another time, after Brookey and Christine had dropped off some furniture and Leroy was putting it in the garage, Chloe saw him sealing a grotesque Halloween mask into a cabinet or a wall. He said it belonged to Brookey and Christine.

She loved him and he was a good husband. He took over all the housework when she went back to school to get a business degree. He was kind and considerate. He wasn't drinking *all* the time.

He had one rule only: Chloe should never associate with Christine because Christine was crazy. She should keep Brookey at a distance too. Chloe would have liked to get together with Leroy's ex-wife and children for holidays, but Leroy explained that they were crazy and not good people.

Whenever Brookey or Travis showed up to discuss something with Leroy, they walked past Chloe, straight into Leroy's office as if Chloe didn't exist.

Only after twenty years of marriage did Chloe see Leroy's frightening side.

Travis Post-Childhood

Chloe did have some contact with Travis. He was not as *persona non grata* as Christine and Brookey were.

Travis was tall and large with long, bushy black hair. He was incapable of holding a job and was often homeless due to his drug addiction.

Chloe: "I don't think he even graduated from the seventh grade. He started using drugs very young, and I think he burned himself out. He did poorly in school, and I just don't think he was very smart. He didn't get it."

Leroy was always trying to help Travis. Brookey could take care of herself but Travis could not. Leroy bought him vehicles, got him flooring jobs, found him apartments. But Travis was too busy partying to take advantage of any of the help.

Leroy started his own flooring business in San Jose – Smith's Floor Covering – so he could hand it over to Travis at some point. Leroy shut it down within a few months and started doing security work.

In the early 1980s, Travis hit bottom. He was in his late twenties or early thirties. He lived on drugs and booze and on the streets. He ate one meal a day at a soup kitchen. He was arrested at least ten times in a period of seven years for public intoxication, loitering, drug related offenses, arson, and attacking an ex-girlfriend during a meth trip.

Brookey West: "My brother liked speed, meth, and he had some guns. He and a friend went over to this gal's house, and they broke in, and she was in bed with this other guy.

So my brother strips them all down naked, and he goes in another room, and he gets this woman's little boy, and he brings him back in, and he says, 'Now you see what a whore your mother is?'"

Someone heard the commotion and called 911. Travis landed in jail.

Brookey continues the story, "By the time he calms down in jail, his hand is broke, his nose is broke, and they were like, what do you expect? So he was going to go to prison for a long time."

He didn't though. Travis was diagnosed as a schizophrenic, judged criminally insane, and sent to Atascadero State Hospital at San Luis Obispo.

Chloe and Leroy visited him there one Christmas. Chloe brought cookies that she had baked for him.

"He came across as a big guy with all this hair," she said, "but to me he just seemed like this big, harmless woolly bear."

Travis cried when Chloe hugged him.

When he was released, Travis went back to the streets. Leroy continued to try to help him get work, but Travis was physically disabled because of his years of doing drugs. At that point, all Leroy could do for him was set up a bank account so Travis could receive his disability checks.

In the early 1990s, Leroy tried one last time to convince Travis to get off the streets and come home. "Dad, I don't want you coming down here anymore," Travis said. "I like living on the street. I've got lots of friends. When you come down here, you just bother me, you disturb me. I don't want you coming down here anymore. I want you to leave me alone."

Christine's Love Life Post-Leroy

In the early 1980s, Christine, now in her early fifties, wanted a man. She came on to workmen and other men, but was always rebuffed. They found her weird. That must have been distressing for someone who had always been so desirable to men.

She honed in on her chiropractor, successful and divorced.

She made a pornographic audio tape of herself masturbating and panting about her love for him. It sounds like a tape intended for someone already involved in a physical relationship with the sender. But the doctor was not remotely interested in Christine.

At one point in the tape, she interrupts the porn for twenty minutes to include a speech from her favorite televangelist who was on TV celebrating the Fourth of July.

According to West, Christine had become obsessed with religious imagery by this time.

After the sermon, Christine's tape goes back to moaning and groaning. She begs the doctor for a secret place for the two of them to be together.

Christine didn't end up giving the tape to the chiropractor because his secretary told her about some other woman the doctor was in love with. The relationship had existed only in Christine's mind, but she was very angry with him.

She told Brookey, "I'm going to get me a gun, and I'm going to shoot that son of a bitch, just like I shot that other one." Brookey refused to get her a gun.

Mother & Daughter Shoplifting Team

Christine and Brookey were caught a few times shoplifting blouses, scarves, and jewelry from high-end department stores. They worked it as a team.

In 1985, Brookey was caught and pleaded guilty to misdemeanor theft and paid a fine. Later that year, when they were arrested after shoplifting together, Christine was upset that the police found Brookey's arrest record but did not find Christine's own conviction record. So she bragged to them about having shot a man.

Mother and daughter were convicted of burglary and conspiracy and sentenced to thirty days in jail and two years of probation.

1993 – Brookey's Third Husband, Howard

In late 1993, Christine and Brookey went to an A.A. meeting at the San Jose Indian Center. Brookey was wearing trampy clothes and Elvira-ish makeup, looking like she wanted to cause trouble. Christine dished out her alcoholic stories and her prison stories and thumped the bible a bit. When the meeting was almost over, Brookey went on a tirade about her ex (West) and how he deserved to be dead.

Everybody at the meeting was afraid of Brookey. Nobody believed the two were Native American.

Later that year, Brookey took up with a man from the Native rehab house next to the Indian Center, Wayne Ike.

Ike said, "She wanted to marry an Indian guy." He loved the sex. But he sensed something was wrong with her. For example, why was this prosperous woman hanging out at a Native rehab center?

Ike also didn't like what she said about kids – she didn't like them and she had given her daughter away. He didn't like how she always talked about money. And he didn't like it when she pulled a gun on him and said, "If I ever catch you messing around, I'll use this on you. If I catch you fucking around, I'll shoot your ass."

Once Ike decided that West was crazy, he hid whenever she came around.

In 1994, Brookey changed her focus to a different man at the halfway house, Howard Simon St. John. She had a good job, a nice car, and a nice house. Howard was a homeless drunk and a drug addict.

Howard's Background

Howard was a child of the South Dakota Sioux, a very noble tribe. He was born on May 15, 1958. He'd had some childhood traumas and been ostracized by his family. He had been drinking regularly since the age of sixteen. His family moved back and forth between South Dakota and California a few times. The last time they left California, Howard dropped out of high school and stayed in California.

He loved partying and he loved booze. He was talented at tweaking cars and often worked for his friend Tony Mercado as a mechanic.

During his mid-twenties, Howard drank until he was unconscious every day. He could down a bottle of tequila. He was also getting into cocaine. He was living on the streets. He already had a huge beer belly and rotten teeth.

By 1988, Howard, aged thirty, was about as low as anybody can go. He'd been arrested for drunk driving, assault and battery, public intoxication, and had been convicted of a felony.

His parole officer wrote that Howard "consumes three to four bottles of hard liquor per week; five cases of beer per week. Drug usage includes peyote during Indian ceremonies only. Cocaine began in 1983. Occasional use. No marks on arms."

Howard's friend Thomas Gutierrez said, "He'd get in fights, he'd get beat up, or he used to get rolled. He would get rolled a lot on the streets. He would pass right out, and people would take his money. He'd be walking downtown, and he would just pass out against a building or something."

In the mid-1980s, Howard found the Native American Indian Center in San Jose and eventually moved in to the halfway house next door. There, Howard lived with eight other end-of-the-line Native alcoholics and started going to Alcoholics Anonymous meetings.

That halfway house is where Howard met Brookey Lee West while Wayne Ike was hiding from her.

Brookey's take on Howard: "When I first met Howard, he looked kind of bad. He was real overweight, and his hair was sort of long. Yet I could see that if he lost some weight and, if he got his hair cut, he would be really good-looking . . . I view life this way – people can be down. They can be sick and they can have a lot of bad things happen, and they can pull themselves back up. That's the way I saw it."

She gave Howard's friends the willies. And they couldn't understand why such a successful woman would want to be with such a loser. They warned him to watch out for an insurance policy.

Howard laughed off his friends' misgivings.

1993 – House In Los Banos, Neighbors On Fir Street, Christine Is Whack

Brookey bought a house on Fir Street in Los Banos in 1993. She brought Christine there to live with her.

Brookey told the neighbors that she had bought the house with a GI loan. She told them that she was a sergeant and that she had flown planes. She also told them the truth, which was that she was a technical writer.

Christine was thin and frail. She had a long braid that hung down to the middle of her back and she always wore a gray sweat suit. Christine made friends with various neighbors. They thought she was lonely and not getting enough nutrition. They found her colorful and interesting but they also thought she was weird and probably insane. Each of them eventually cut themselves off from her.

Christine told the neighbors that she was a strong Cherokee woman who would not take guff from anyone. She talked about being from Ennis and riding the rails with hobos at the age of twelve and pulling a knife on them when they got fresh. She talked about how her granddaughter had been kidnapped from a department store. She gave them bizarre gifts. One was a pair of earrings made out of potatoes.

People who visited Christine saw a room in the house that contained a rack of clothes with the price tags still on them. Some visitors wondered if the reason all those clothes were in the house was because Brookey was running prostitutes. They only had Brookey's say-so that she was a tech writer in Silicon Valley.

Christine would walk into somebody's house unannounced. She and Brookey tried to sell a car to a neighbor for twice what it was worth. Christine brought a neighbor some soup that tasted like pure salt. She claimed she could make love potions.

Christine was proud of her violent history. She bragged about shooting a man in Bakersfield. She said she had been on Death Row until the man came back to life in the morgue. The neighbors knew that was impossible.

Neighbor Laura Parra thought that Brookey looked creepy and might be on drugs.

Everybody could see and hear mother and daughter screaming at each other. They heard Brookey calling her mother a crazy bitch. Brookey told Laura that she didn't like her mother.

Laura: "Brooke said her mom was a lunatic, she was driving her crazy and she didn't want her mom around . . . she talked about what a pain in the ass her mother was, and her exact words were, 'She's a crazy bitch, and I can't wait to get her out.'"

1994 – Brookey Marries Howard

Howard moved into Brookey's new house early in 1994. Whatever good habits had rubbed off on him at the halfway house were gone. He was drinking again. He drove the neighbors around the bend. He stumbled around drunk out of his mind. He was noisy and rude, he slammed doors, he looked ragged, and the neighbors often heard cursing and bottles breaking.

Some tried to interact with him, but Howard was shy and usually wasted.

A few homes on the street were burgled after Howard moved in, and the neighbors wondered if Howard and Brookey were involved.

His father would not let him get married on the reservation in South Dakota, so Howard and Brookey were married in Reno on April 30. Brookey showed Howard's friends a $20,000 ring that Howard had bought for her, but his friends knew that she had to have bought it for herself.

In their collective opinion, Howard was playing with fire.

Christine and Howard could not stand each other and fought constantly. Brookey bought Christine a van, drove her with her possessions to Santa Clara, parked the van in a parking lot, and told Christine not to come back. According to Leroy, that seemed normal in the relationship dynamic between Brookey and Christine.

Back on Fir Street, Sandy Corona started a Neighborhood Watch program. The only people in the neighborhood not invited to the first meeting on May 21, 1994, were Brookey and Howard. The next day, Sandy found a pile of crushed ice in front of her door. Down the street, she saw Howard toasting her with a bottle of Coke. Sandy was terrified of Howard.

There seemed to be more patrol cars around since Howard had moved in. Sometimes the police visited Brookey's house and the neighbors wondered if it had something to do with the clothes that looked stolen. They wonder if Brookey was a drug dealer. And the husband was always loaded.

Howard's friends continued to worry about him. They knew he didn't fit in where he was living. They didn't trust Brookey.

They visited him in the spring of 1994 and they loved the place. They left within an hour. They didn't like being around Brookey.

Burning The Jaguar

A few weeks later, Howard visited his friends. He told them that Brookey wanted him to burn the Jag for insurance money and he asked his friend Thomas Gutierrez to help him. Gutierrez refused, saying that it would be too easy for the cops to get evidence.

On the night of March 3, 1994, an anonymous caller reported a car fire to 911. When the police showed up to the dirt road, they found a burning 1989 Jaguar – a write-off.

Brookey reported her Jaguar missing about fifty minutes later.

She claimed the car had disappeared while she and her boyfriend were at dinner and a movie. The insurance company paid out $18,897. But they were suspicious about the fire and hired a private investigator to look into it.

Days after the Jag burned, Howard showed up in a Corvette to visit his friends. He told them it was a wedding gift from Brookey. Eventually he admitted to Gutierrez that he had burned the Jag. He said he was nervous because the insurance company was sniffing around.

Howard had just married a woman he hardly knew. Now he was committing crimes for her. Gutierrez again expressed his grave concerns that being involved with Brookey was dangerous for Howard.

The neighbors on Fir Street saw Howard tinkering with the Corvette. When they asked where Brookey's Jag was, they were told that it had been stolen, stripped, and burned.

Dwight Bell was the investigator hired by the insurance company. He later gave authorities a laundry list of suspicious circumstances about the Jag: the car was reported missing *after* it was found burning, everything that is worth stealing from a car was intact, none of the normal causes of car fires were involved, and he had found metal distortion indicative of the involvement of a flammable liquid.

By May 1994, Bell was sure the car had been torched for the insurance money, but he couldn't get in touch with Brookey and he didn't have much actual evidence.

Brookey Shoots Howard

On May 21, 1994, the people of Fir Street saw Howard and Brookey looking very cozy. Mike Stoykovich from across the street saw them hugging and kissing in the garage. Laura and Fermin Parra saw them dancing and embracing in the garage.

At some point, Howard went over to ask Fermin why people didn't like him and Brookey. He wondered if it was Christine's fault. Howard was very drunk. Fermin was polite but went back into his house as soon as he could and told his family to keep away from the St. Johns.

Later that day, the people of Fir Street heard a gunshot. Some thought it was a door slamming and some thought it was a firecracker. They heard yelling. Then they saw Howard stumbling out of the garage covered with blood and screaming, "She shot me!" Someone ran into Parra's house and called 911.

The police officer who responded saw that Howard had a bullet wound on his neck. He heard from Brookey, "I did shoot him, but it was an accident." He heard from Howard, "Bitch, you shot me. I'm going to kill you." Brookey said that Howard was coming at her so she took her .32 out of her purse and pointed it at him, and it "just went off." Brookey said that she called 911.

Howard was taken away in an ambulance and Brookey was taken away in handcuffs.

Brookey told police that they were cleaning the garage when Howard became aggressive. She said there had been a series of domestic disputes before this. During this one, he was obsessing that she might be leaving him. He wanted to have sex on the concrete floor of the garage. She did not want to do that. He threw a table at her. She took the gun out of her purse and it accidentally went off.

She didn't give the police a good reason why her .32 was in her purse while her other guns were locked up. She didn't give them a reason why she had her purse in the garage.

According to Howard's statement to police, Brookey said to him, "I'm setting you up." When the police asked him why she would do such a thing, he told them, "She's a crazy bitch."

Brookey was charged with felony assault with a gun and corporal injury to a spouse. The charges were dropped two weeks later on May 25.

Howard had been flown to a hospital in Modesto. He had a big hole in his neck but no artery had been damaged. The doctors decided to leave the .32 bullet in his left shoulder.

Howard phoned the insurance investigators from his hospital room. He admitted to burning the Jaguar and told them that Brookey had given him a Corvette as payment.

Within a week, Howard was released from the hospital. He visited his old friends. He told Mercado and Gutierrez that Brookey had ambushed him in the garage. She told Howard she was going to kill him because the insurance people were getting suspicious. She said she was going to burn the house down.

Back on Fir Street, Leroy showed up in front of Brookey's house. He talked to neighbor Mike Stoykovich about Brookey's troubles and said how disappointed he was that she had married an Indian. He also said a few racist things about Indians.

He told Stoykovich he had no plans to get her out of jail until she calmed down.

A couple of days later Brookey was out on her own recognizance and Leroy dropped her off on Fir Street.

Brookey told her neighbors that she was afraid of Howard, that she was getting a restraining order and a Rottweiler dog, and that the shooting had been in self-defense because Howard was throwing things at her.

Howard Goes Back To Brookey

It seemed that the Howard and Brookey saga was over. He'd reported her to the insurance people and she'd had a restraining order placed against him. But within a few weeks Brookey told him she would sign the cars and house over to him if he came back. He did.

Howard's friends told him he was crazy. They told him she would kill him. He just had nowhere else to go.

The insurance investigator, Bell, eventually found Howard. He was very drunk, sitting on a bench outside a hospital where he was scheduled to have treatment for his neck wound. While Bell talked to him, Howard chugged a couple of airplane bottles of tequila and chased them with Coke.

He told Bell he had already snorted ½ a gram of meth and drunk six or seven airplane bottles of tequila.

Howard told Bell that he made up the whole story about doing the arson to punish Brookey for shooting him. He gave Bell the original alibi about dinner and a movie. He talked about Brookey's work and his own hernia. He claimed that Brookey had to shoot him because he was slapping her around.

Later he admitted to his friend Tyla Knotchapone that if he'd never met Brookey he wouldn't have a bullet in his neck. "I just want to forget her. She is bad news. I think she's going to kill me," Howard told her.

According to Tyla, "He was in tears, actually. He said, 'I can't believe I have this kind of problem in my life with a woman. This woman is dangerous, Tyla. I don't know how to go about divorcing her. It's like she's got me in a web, and I know the way out, but I'm scared. What could be next? I'm scared to find out.'"

Howard described to Tyla how Brookey abused her mother physically and verbally. After offering him a room at her place, Tyla asked him why he'd gone back to Brookey.

"I'm so stupid," he said. "I don't know why."

Brookey Goes Missing

On June 2, 1994, Brookey ran out into the middle of Fir Street shouting that Howard was threatening to kill her because she had misplaced their wedding photo. The police took her to a coffee shop and she told them she was going to divorce him.

Howard, worried about her, spent the next two days looking for her. He filed a missing persons report on June 4. He thought Brookey had been kidnapped. He pestered the police, but they believed she was voluntarily missing. Howard made some frantic drunken calls to Leroy who assured him that he shouldn't worry about her. Leroy disconnected his phone to get some sleep.

That night, Howard told one of his halfway house friends on the phone that he might have to kill her to get even with her.

Howard Is Shot Dead

Sometime in the twenty-four hours following Howard's last phone conversation, he was shot in the back and his body was dumped near the Tule River in Sequoia National Forest, several hours' drive away from Fir Street.

He wasn't murdered there. He was dumped there like garbage.

Howard's body was discovered in the Forest on June 6, sixteen days after Brookey shot him in the neck and three months after he torched the Jag for her. He had been shot in the back with a .38 handgun.

The police report describes him as a former parolee with eight aliases and fifteen misdemeanors, thirty-five years old, 230 lbs.

It was a sad end to a sad life. People had loved Howard Simon St. John and had hoped that he could turn things around. They will continue to miss him.

When police called Howard's father, Sylvester (no longer disowning him) told them that Howard had been in rehab in San Jose for addiction, that he was married to a woman who lived in Los Banos, and that they had a domestic abuse history.

This led investigators to Brookey.

Brookey had been living in a motel after she left Howard. On June 4, she had picked up Christine at her van in Santa Clara and taken her shopping all day. She went to Silicon Valley to work that night – as a contractor she could work whatever hours she wanted – and the door system showed that she had carded her way in.

Christine and Brookey claimed that Howard had found $3,000 in cash in the house and taken off to Reno to party with friends.

They said that when they returned to the house it was a shambles and that it was full of evidence that people other than Howard had been there that night.

Brookey's story about the whole weekend was full of holes, but investigators were never able to find enough hard evidence to bring charges against her.

Howard's lifestyle offered many other possibilities for why he would have been murdered. Christine herself was a suspect for a while. Investigators believe that, if Brookey did it, both of her parents would have helped her cover it up. The case is officially open to this day.

Thus ended Brookey's third short marriage.

Chloe Sees Leroy's Bad Side

Leroy was diagnosed with brain cancer in 1995 and had a stroke in 1996.

In 1995, Chloe discovered that Leroy had forged her name on twenty-five credit card applications and almost $250,000 in cash advances from those had disappeared. She thought Leroy had given it to Brookey, but Brookey insisted that he had gambled it away.

Chloe also suspected that Brookey had been meddling with Leroy's finances so she would get everything when he died. In early 1996, Brookey told Chloe that she and Leroy had given away his gun collection to pay off thousands of dollars he owed to bookies.

In February 1996, Chloe was looking under Leroy's bed for the titles to six vehicles owned by her and Leroy when Brookey tried to zap her with a stun gun and then tried to hit her with it. Leroy jumped out of his bed and screamed at Chloe that she was a trouble-making bitch. Chloe ran to the parking lot with Brookey chasing her and screaming at her. When Chloe called the police, Brookey drove away.

Leroy told the police that Chloe's story was a lie. Chloe believes that Brookey was trying to kill her and that Leroy was in on it. If Chloe died, Leroy would get $250,000 life insurance which would then go to Brookey when Leroy died. Leroy died two months later.

Thus ended Chloe's marriage with the new and improved Leroy.

Brookey's Fourth Marriage Fizzles: George Burnette

George Burnette, another Native American, looked much like Howard St. John though his black hair hung down to his waist. Burnette and West met in November 1996 at a casino in Las Vegas. Their whirlwind passionate romance began when they spent Thanksgiving Day together.

They were married on January 7, 1997 in Las Vegas.

Within a day of arriving at Brookey's Los Banos house, Brookey told George that she had to go back to Las Vegas to be with her sick mother. The next thing he knew was that Brookey and her car were gone.

He drove to Christine's new apartment in Las Vegas and found that she knew nothing of the marriage. Soon the marriage was annulled. Burnette testified to West's instability at her trial.

Christine Gets A Las Vegas Apartment

In 1997, when Christine was sixty-five, Brookey set her up in a low-rent apartment in Las Vegas. The place was called Orange Door. Christine was still into Jesus and still lying about having Native heritage and still bragging about having been on Death Row for shooting a man. Christine had osteoporosis. Alzheimer's was creeping up on her.

But she became close friends with some of her neighbors. One of them, Alice Wilsey, sixty-six, looked after Christine when Brookey was in California.

Another neighbor, Judy Chang, seventy-four, also enjoyed Christine's company.

Brookey visited often and then moved in with her mother in late 1997. Christine's friends could see that the two loved each other but they also saw the two had bitter arguments.

At some point in 1997, Brookey went AWOL from her job at Hybrid Networks. She had checked herself into a psychiatric hospital. After she got out, she confided more and more in a co-worker, Natalie Hanke.

She told Hanke about a big burglary ring she had once been part of, an exaggeration of her shoplifting escapades with Christine. She told her about Howard's murder and said that she could have done it if someone hadn't beaten her to it. She said her father was a powerful warlock. She talked about how much she hated her mother and what a sociopath and psychopath and financial drain she was. She said that she was going to send her mother to live with Travis who was also a sociopath. They would get along well.

Christine Disappears

Christine was quite sick, bedridden most of the time. The last time Wilsey saw Christine, Brookey was giving her pills, supposedly aspirin. Two days later, Brookey told Chang that Christine had gone to live with Travis in San Jose. This was in February 1998.

West said she had told Christine her only other options were being put in a home or West leaving her there and never coming back. She had driven her to San Jose in the middle of the night, she said.

Christine's friends noticed things that made them suspicious about Brookey's story. They saw some of Christine's possessions in the dumpster. They saw her most prized possessions still in the apartment and believed that Christine would definitely have taken them with her.

On November 11, 1998, Wilsey wrote a letter to the police listing six reasons why she thought Christine had met with foul play. She added that she had witnessed Brookey's violence and mental instability. She outright accused West of killing her mother in a rage. She asked the police to look into Christine's bank account and Social Security checks. She added that she herself was afraid of West.

When she brought the letter to the police, they asked her to come back another day but she never did. She knew that she could be wrong about the entire thing.

Brookey continued to talk about her mother as if she was still a pain in the ass for the whole three years after Christine's friends had last seen her until police discovered Christine's body in the garbage bin.

Natalie Hanke distanced herself from Brookey as she saw more of Brookey's weird side. Brookey continued to rage about her mother. Her Las Vegas apartment was full of weird voodoo-ish things that Brookey claimed were her mother's. The one time Hanke was there, she pretended to be sick just to get away.

Hanke had lunch with Brookey one last time in 1999 during a trip to Las Vegas. Brookey then tried to lure her to the storage locker. Hanke now believes that West was planning to kill her and steal her identity.

Brookey Lee's Luck Comes To An End

In 1985, nobody suspected Brookey or Leroy of any involvement in the shooting of Veramontes' grandmother. In 1985, Brookey and Christine got off with fines and probation for shoplifting. In 1994, it couldn't be proved that Brookey had committed insurance fraud, charges of spousal abuse were dropped, and Howard's murder couldn't be pinned on her. In 1996, she wasn't charged with trying to stun gun her stepmother Chloe.

Then on February 8, 2001, Christine's mostly liquefied body was discovered in the garbage can in the storage unit and identified through dental records.

As the storage locker was in West's name, police got a warrant to search her apartment. They found a key for the storage locker. They found duct tape. They found bank statements showing that $30,000 of Social Security checks in Christine's name had been cashed over the years.

Investigators were not able to catch Brookey at home. But a few days into the investigation, Detective Dave Mesinar saw Brookey's plate number on her truck at a 7-11. Then he saw her inside the store.

On February 8, Brookey was arrested, charged with murder, and taken to Clark County Detention Center without making a statement. She had babbled her face off while being interrogated in the Howard St. John cases.

The next day, she was interviewed by a TV news anchor and said that her mother had died of natural causes and she had put her in the trash bin rather than report the death. This made things easier for Mesinar, because he would not have to look for other suspects.

West's involvement was further confirmed when a single print of hers was found on the plastic that sealed the trash can.

The Investigation

Mesinar received information from Daniel Haynes, an investigator in Howard's murder case, and found out that there had been a plastic bag partially on Howard's face when his body was found.

Haynes gave Mesinar a lot of other information about Brookey's life and background. Mesinar concluded that she was certainly capable of killing.

Investigators and the prosecutor Frank Coumou believed Brookey had killed her mother for the money, out of hatred, and because commuting between Las Vegas and San Jose was inconvenient.

Mesinar and his team dug in and interviewed all the people who had known Brookey and Christine. They spent weeks looking for Brookey's brother Travis but, like Haynes before them, they couldn't find him alive or dead. They did find out that around the time Travis was last seen alive Brookey had written to Social Security to have Travis' checks deposited into an account that she had access to.

Mesinar realized that, if Brookey had killed her mother, her husband, and her brother, she was a serial killer. (It has never been proved that West killed St. John and it has never been proved that Travis Lee Smith is dead.)

The medical examiner wasn't able to confirm that Christine was murdered. Her body was too decomposed. But the pathologists were able to prove murder through maggot evidence.

If Christine had been found dead and then put in the bin, as Brookey claimed, the maggots would have been from blowflies. Blowflies find their way to a corpse almost instantly. But the maggots were from coffin flies not blowflies, indicating that Christine's body had been sealed into the bin before blowflies had a chance to find her body.

Investigators thought it was likely that Christine was still alive when she was sealed in the bin. The lack of blowflies certainly proved pre-meditation.

Trial & Conviction

West pleaded not guilty at a preliminary hearing. The trial began on July 6, 2001.

Brookey's defense continued to be that her mother had a lot of medical problems and died of natural causes. Evidence about Christine's medical history was presented at trial. Brookey discovered Christine's body and put her in the bin so she wouldn't have to deal with police. She was still a suspect in Howard's murder and wanted no involvement with them in relation to yet another death.

She didn't deny spending her mother's checks and the prosecution presented evidence that somebody, probably Brookey, had been cashing them.

The prosecution argued that the motives were hatred and money. After reading Brookey's books from the storage locker, Coumou developed a theory involving Satanism that dovetailed with the way Christine's body had been disposed and the plastic bag on her face. But he left that theory out of the trial, worried about future appeals.

The prosecution tore apart the "living with Travis" story because he'd been homeless and then missing for years. If the jury believed that Christine had been living with Travis for some of the past three years, it would shoot down the idea that Brookey had Christine in the storage locker and was cashing her checks the entire time.

Travis had last been seen in 1993. His last known mailing address was the Los Banos house that Brookey and Christine had lived in. His disability checks were cut off in 1999 when administrators couldn't get in touch with him. His driver's license had been expired for ages.

The judge did not allow the prosecution to hint that Travis might be dead, though prosecutors suspected that Brookey had killed him for his checks.

A slew of witnesses, including West's fourth husband and Natalie Hanke, testified about West's personality.

Closing arguments took place on July 18. It took the jury two hours to find Brookey Lee West guilty of first degree murder. The primary reasons for the conviction were the plastic bag around Christine's face and the maggots being the wrong kind of maggots.

Sentence

In September 1994, Judge Mosley sentenced Brookey Lee West to life without parole. He firmly believed that

Christine had been deliberately suffocated with the plastic bag.

"We've heard two possible explanations. One is that it was a shroud . . . in deference to the decedent's status. And, of course, we've heard the other suggestion – that it was, in essence, what killed her by virtue of suffocating.

"I have to tell you, Ms. West, that the latter is more likely in my view. She was overpowered, this item placed around her face, tied tightly, and she was placed into this garbage container, presumably to suffocate her . . ."

Mosely finished with, "While I think everyone would agree putting someone's mother in a garbage can to bury her is bizarre, placing her in there conscious to suffocate her is not only bizarre – it's criminal. You are sentenced to life without the possibility of parole. That's all."

Appeals

Brookey unsuccessfully appealed her conviction in 2003. Her side argued that a natural death due to medical issues had not been disproved. The appeal Justices said that the circumstances "clearly created a reasonable inference of Smith's death by criminal agency."

The Justices also rejected her lawyer's argument that Judge Mosley had erred in admitting photographs of the victim. They opined that gruesome photos have to be allowed if they help with "ascertaining the truth" and these photos helped jurors to see the importance of the plastic bag.

In 2004, Brookey had hopes of a new trial when it was discovered that a man using her brother's name and Social

Security number had been to the Santa Clara Medical Center in San Jose. Investigators weren't able to track this person down. There is a possibility that this person, Travis or not, moved on to Florida. Nobody ever found him.

Finding Travis wouldn't have helped Brookey though. Her trial jury had heard a recording of her saying, "No one knows where he is and no one has seen him in years," which flew in the face of her claim that Christine had been living with him.

In appealing her sentence in 2006, her lawyer argued that she would have been handed a lighter sentence if Veramontes' evidence about being intimidated with Satanic threats had not been presented.

The Supreme Court of Nevada ruled that she was "not sentenced by virtue of some mistreatment that [she] foisted upon Mr. Veramontes." The judge "felt the evidence was overwhelming as to [her] guilt."

Prison

Brookey Lee West is serving her sentence in the Florence McClure Women's Correctional Center near Las Vegas. She is a model prisoner. She leads a Bible study class. She teaches art. She helps raise awareness and money to help Nevada's wild horses.

She denies involvement in any crimes except shoplifting. She does admit that Leroy sent the threatening letter to her daughter's father. She says that in 1999 she was bringing her mother back from Travis to Las Vegas and her mother died in a hotel room on the way.

In 2008 she was sending product to a man who sells murderabilia online. He sold some of her art and some t-shirts that she had worn and signed. He didn't find a buyer for her fingernail clippings at $19.95.

In July 2012 Brookey attempted a prison break. She changed her appearance and tried to walk out while the inmates were heading to breakfast. Staff recognized her standing near a security gate, right next to the main exit/entrance.

Judge Donald Mosley said in a TV interview: "It was one of the most bizarre trials I've had in my now thirty years on the bench . . . I never saw one iota of remorse . . . I think, all things considered, Brookey West got exactly what she deserved."

A SERIAL KILLER'S ROAD TRIP

Nathan Nixon

The 1950's for the United States of America is best remembered as some of the most trying times in the history of the nation. While the early 1950's saw the baby boom, the late half of the decade was marred by civil instability and mistrust. Many Americans, especially those in the southern United States, lost their trust in the American dream as well as the government. Many of those Americans took their destiny into their own hands.

Charles Starkweather may have been the epitome of the decline of human morals in the late 1950's. In one of the most notable murder sprees in the modern era, Hollywood has recreated the life of Charles Starkweather many times over.

Charles Starkweather is best known for a murder spree that spanned over the course of just a few months. The circumstances surrounding this reign of terror make it unique to the crime community.

Charles Raymond "Charlie" Starkweather was born on November 24, 1938 in the rural city of Lincoln, Nebraska. As was common in the earlier eras of the 20th century, Starkweather was a part of a large family. He was the third of seven siblings to be born. While he was not especially close to his siblings, he shared a normal relationship with each of them with all factors considered.

Guy Starkweather was Charles' father. Guy fit in with most any southern male at the time. He was a hard-working southern man who took great pride in supporting his family the best that he could. Just after Charles was born, the United States entered into World War II. Due to severe rheumatoid arthritis, Guy was not able to serve his country in the war. While many young children were losing their fathers to the war effort in this era, Charles was lucky enough to have his father at home. Also due to Guy's severe rheumatoid arthritis, he was often unable to complete his work as a carpenter. When Guy was not having a medical flare up of his arthritis, he was well-known in the community as a great wood worker who could complete seemingly any task. However, Guy's condition ultimately led to the Starkweather family living a poor life financially, even by rural standards.

Charles' mother was named Helen Starkweather. Helen was the picture of what a mother should be. She went out of her way to stay active and involved in each of her children's lives. When Guy Starkweather would suffer a flare up and be left unable to work, she would supplement the household income by waitressing. Helen was able to balance this work along with her work at home with taking care of seven children. Helen and Charles shared a good relationship, although he would later admit that he felt "forgotten" as he grew in to his teenage years with so many younger siblings in the house.

Overall, Charles held great memories of his childhood. Unlike most of the killers in the 20th century, he had a strong relationship with his family. Beyond a financially poor situation for most of his childhood, the love and family bond in the home was a great situation for a child to be around.

Charles Starkweather did not share the same happy memories of his education as he did of his family life. He was one of those students who changed drastically from his elementary and middle school years to his high school years. The change was most drastic on his classmates, who could quickly see that Charles was hiding anger from his early years.

A look into the elementary and middle school years of Charles reveals much to behold on some sort of explanation as to why he would carry such a burden. Charles notable had a severe speech impediment. His parents were well aware, even in his toddler years, that his speech was quite different than the rest of his siblings. Financial burdens prevented any sort of speech therapy that could help Charles work through his problem. Throughout his elementary and middle school years, he was bullied nearly every day by his classmates. He would find himself at the center of mean jokes. It was strongly due to this fact that Charles struggled socially at an early age. Many of the other students came after him for being different.

Charles' speech impediment was not the only difference he shared with most of his other classmates. Charles also was born with a condition called genu varum. Genu varum is a birth defect that causes legs to be misshapen in a variety of ways. While individuals with this condition learn to cope and eventually even out as they develop more fully, it was yet another source of bullying that Charles endured. With a speech impediment and a birth defect that affected the look of his legs, Charles Starkweather endured treatment from his classmates that no child should have to endure. Even at a young age, Charles learned quickly that people could be mean.

Even through the bullying in his younger years, Charles Starkweather surprisingly showed no signs of lashing out at his classmates. He more or less took the bullying in stride. While he had very few friends and companions outside of his family, he was an alarmingly quiet child at school.

As Charles entered into his late middle school years, a change became evident in Charles. Charles attended Irving Junior High. It is here that many stories of Charles begin in an attempt to explain a possible motive for his actions. Educationally, Charles struggled tremendously in school. He had a hard time staying focused in many of his core subject classes. Upon beginning his junior high years at Irving, his school problems began to grow. There was one subject, however, that Charles excelled at. Starkweather blossomed in physical education.

Like most other boys his age, Charles was beginning to see his body change. The changes in his body, however, were much more rapid and noticeable than most of his other classmates. Charles was among the tallest and most impressive bodied students in the entire school. The once quiet student who endured more than his fair share of bullies in his elementary years now discovered something. He was bigger than everyone else.

That quiet student who had few friends was not the scared, unassuming boy that many of his teachers and classmates felt that he was. In reality, Charles took note of each student who had bullied him growing up. That is not to say that he had a "list" or anything along those lines. However, he knew that how he was being treated wasn't right. More importantly, he knew that he didn't like it.

Charles Starkweather took gym class as a time to 'get back' at all of those students who had treated him so poorly in his younger years. He would frequently get in fights and make fun of students around him. It took no time at all for Charles' reputation to change. Once considered one of the nicest, most well-behaved students in the school district, he was now considered the "bad child" who didn't fear consequence. Apart from a small circle of friends he gained in junior high and high school, many of the students feared Charles. Most of the students did their best to avoid him at all cost. Bob von Busch, one of his select few friends from his childhood, best sums up the change that everyone noticed in Charles.

"He could be the kindest person you have ever seen. He would actually do anything for you if he found a way to like you. He was a hell of a lot of fun to be around, too. Everything was just one big joke to him. His actions would bring that attitude out in the small group of friends he surrounded himself with. But, he had this other side. A darker side. He could be mean as hell. Just downright cruel. If he saw some poor guy on the street who was bigger than he was, maybe better looking than he was, or better dressed, he would try to take the poor bastard down to his size."

With the change in the personality of Charles Starkweather, it was only a matter of time for more changes to happen. It wouldn't be until Charles turned 17 that the next major change would happen for Charles.

When Charles entered his senior year at 17 years old, his reputation had not changed. While he had a strong circle of friends with whom he had, arguably, too much fun with, he still had the same issues that he previously possessed. He struggled mightily in school, notably lacking any sort of motivation in his studies. Charles didn't do well with authority, either. For this and several other reasons, he would drop out of school just one year short of graduating. He would go on to get his first real job at a Western Union newspaper warehouse. While it didn't pay much money, it offered Charles a chance to get out of the school environment that he hated so much.

In 1956, at just 18 years old, Charles Starkweather would meet the person that would change his life forever. The grounds for their meeting is odd in itself. Charles was introduced to a young, 13-year-old girl named Caril Ann Fugate. Charles was dating Caril's older sister at the time of their introduction. Strangely enough, the two became quite close, often confiding in each other with long talks and intimacy. Shortly after, Charles ended his relationship with Caril's sister. Immediately thereafter, Caril Ann Fugate and Charles Starkweather began their relationship.

Charles' job was located right next to the junior high that Caril attended. He would go be with her each and every day after school. He was considered a terrible employee. His employer described Starkweather just after his murder conviction.

"Sometimes you'd have to tell him the same thing two or three times. Even then, he may not do what he was told because he didn't want to be told. Other times, he struggled understanding basic commands. He was by far the dumbest man we had there."

Caril's and Charles' relationship caused major rifts and consequences and both of their families. It was early in 1957 that Starkweather decided to teach Caril how to drive. He allowed her to drive his 1949 Ford. She quickly crashed the car into another vehicle early one morning. The owner of the Ford, however, was not Charles, but his father Guy. Guy agreed to pay the damages with money that he could hardly spare. This was the breaking point for Guy Starkweather. He banished Charles from the family home and ordered him to never return. With dropping out of school, dating a 13-year-old girl, and crashing the family car, Guy had had enough. Charles, greatly angry at the whole situation, agreed to leave.

Caril's family strongly disapproved of her relationship as well. Obviously, it didn't sit well at all with her parents that she was admittedly dating an 18-year-old boy who had a reputation as a trouble maker. Moreover, at just 13 years old, they felt it was entirely inappropriate for her to be with him in any fashion.

Charles' life was now making another major turn. He was hired on as a garbage collector. He would make minimum wage and struggle to get by for the next several months. But this job had a greater impact than what appears on the surface. During the routes, Charles began to form highly nihilistic views. These views basically meant that whatever circumstance he was currently in was how he was destined to live his life. This was an extremely negative view. He had been in poverty his entire life, and seeing his life turn to working a garbage route for minimum wage helped push him to this gloomy outlook.

Also on these routes, Charles began to plan different robberies. He strongly believed that the best way to change his fortune was to 'take what he wanted'. It was during this time that he would form his famous philosophy on life: "Dead people are all on the same level." He would live the rest of his life by this philosophy. He was not at all shy about this fact either. During his trial, he affirmed this philosophy many times. This officially would mark the beginning of a reign of terror.

The story of Charles Starkweather's murder spree is impossible to tell without understanding the relationship between him and Fugate. To Charles, Caril was his best friend, his partner in crime. She happily went along with whatever he wanted. She readily broke the rules to be with him. He admired that about her. Charles Starkweather always had something to prove. To most of the investigators surrounding the case, Caril likely gave Charles the confidence and motivation to begin his awful streak. Charles was even able to convince Caril to run away with him. While Caril Ann Fugate denies any knowledge of the murders that Charles would commit beforehand, many believe that Charles convinced Caril to murder her whole family. That fact, however, has never officially been proven.

The circumstance that surrounds Charles' first murder is nothing special all things considered. He didn't have ties to the person he murdered. It wasn't a past childhood acquaintance or even someone that he knew. A late November evening would start one of the most notorious murder sprees in recent history.

In the late hours of November 30, 1957, Charles Starkweather entered a service station in his hometown of Lincoln, Nebraska. Starkweather initially intended to buy a stuffed animal as a gift for Caril. However, he wanted to make the purchase on credit. The clerk that evening, Robert Colvert, refused to complete the sale. Charles became enraged as he stormed out of the store. Charles Starkweather would return to the store three times over the next several hours. He made small purchases. Colvert was disturbed at the awkward behavior of Starkweather.

Finally, Charles Starkweather entered the storm carrying a shotgun. An intense struggle ensued over the gun in which Colvert was injured. Starkweather forced Colvert into his car where he drove him to an extremely remote area on the edge of town. Starkweather forced Colvert out of the car, where he robbed him of $100. After another struggle, Starkweather fired a single shot at point blank range into Robert Colvert's head. With this single shot, Charles Starkweather had committed his first murder.

Charles quickly drove back to Caril Ann Fugate. He confessed to her that he had robbed the service station. However, he foolishly denied actually killing Colvert. He professed to Fugate that someone else had killed Colvert.

During the investigation after the murder spree, Fugate admitted that she didn't believe Starkweather. She knew fully that he had, indeed, murdered Colvert. She claimed that she only went along with the story out of fear of Starkweather. Police, however, never believed that she feared Charlie. Their strong suspicion was that the story and potential for what they were to do was a source of excitement for Caril.

During his murder trial, Starkweather made several eerie sentiments regarding this first murder.

"I had transcended my former self. I reached a new plane of existence in which I was outside the law and could commit any crime without guilt or fear of repercussion."

At this point, Caril and Charles knew that it was only a matter of time before word got around that Charles was, indeed, the killer. This first murder would set off a chain of events that were both devastating and, as the timeline will show, extremely fast.

On January 21, 1958, Starkweather hurried off to the home of Caril Fugate. Caril was not home. Fugate's mother and stepfather, Velda and Marion Bartlett, were at the residence. As was known to Charles, they tried everything that they could to separate Charles and Caril. Caril's parents and Charles Starkweather did not get along. When Charles Starkweather began yelling at them and shouting obscenities, they ordered him to leave the premises and to stay away from Caril. Charles, however, had other plans.

Starkweather returned to his car, and came back to the home with the same shotgun from his first murder. He walked right in the front door and shot both Velda and Marion Bartlett at point blank range. Sadly, they would not be the only two people murdered that afternoon.

Also inside the home was the two-year-old daughter of Velda and Marion Bartlett. Little Billie Jean Bartlett was crying relentlessly at the noise and disturbance in the home. Charles Starkweather proceeded to strangle and stab the innocent Billie Jean. Of all the victims of the murder spree, this is by far the most disturbing.

Caril Ann Fugate would arrive at the home less than one hour later. Upon her arrival, Charles and Caril hid the gruesome bodies of Caril's family behind the house. Great debate has long been had as to the circumstance of this murder. While most everyone believes that Caril and Charles agreed to kill her family as a way for her to be able to flee with him, Caril vehemently denied this fact. She claims that she never intended for her family to be murdered, but that she had no choice but to go along with it after Charles murdered them.

Eerily enough, the couple remained in the house until January 27. With the bodies of her family less than 50 feet away, Caril stayed in the home with Charles. It was only after Caril's grandmother became worried that police were notified that something was happening. This spooked Charles and Caril. It was only then did they decide to hit the road.

Fugate and Starkweather entered into his car and fled the home. They intended to leave Lincoln altogether. Many argue that the murder spree was not planned. Based on Charles behavior and mental state as described after his first murder, most think that he was acting on instinct after the Bartlett murders.

The couple fled on January 27, 1958 to Bennet, Nebraska. They drove to a secluded farmhouse of 70-year-old August Meyer. Meyer was a family friend of the Starkweather family. He was a trusted member of the local community that was known for his blue-collar work ethic and his willingness to help anyone. When Caril and Charles arrived at his home, he never gave a second thought to allowing them to enter his home. Upon entering the home, Charles revealed his shotgun. He quickly fired two powerful blast to the head of August Meyer. For no apparent reason, Charles Starkweather also decided to kill Meyer's dog. The 5th victim of the Starkweather murder spree had just been claimed.

The couple spent no time at all at the Meyer house. They took a few valuables and quickly fled the area. Several miles outside of Bennet, Starkweather managed to get their car stuck in the mud on the side of a rural dirt road. Two local teenagers, Robert Jensen and Carol King, came upon their car and offered their help to free the car. When they exited the vehicle, Starkweather brandished his shotgun and forced them to back to their car at gun point. He made them drive Caril and himself back into Bennet. They arrived to an abandoned storm shelter. After they had exited the vehicle, Robert Jensen was shot in the back of the head with the shotgun. Charles then attempted to rape Carol King. King fought with everything she had and was able to hold him off. Frustrated by this, Starkweather shot King in the chest with the barrel just inches away from her body.

During the investigation after his arrest, Starkweather admitted to shooting Jensen, but claimed that Fugate was the one to actually shoot King. While this has never been proven, many believe there is merit to this claim. It is often concluded that Fugate was frustrated that Starkweather had tried to rape King. Upon coming upon the struggle, it is claimed that she picked up the shotgun and fired the shot that killed Carol King.

The couple's next move was to return to Lincoln. Upon entering town, they drove straight to one of the richest neighborhoods in the area. It was here that they entered the home of wealthy industrialist C. Lauer Ward. Lauer was not home, however his wife and their maid were. When the couple entered the home, they immediately stabbed Lauer's wife Clara as well as the housekeeper. To add further death to the scene, Starkweather snapped the family dog's neck, killing it instantly.

Several hours later, C. Lauer Ward returned home. Upon walking in the back door, Starkweather was waiting for him with his shotgun. Less than three feet into his home, Ward was shot in the head and killed. Caril and Charles then took all of the valuables in the house that they could find. This included jewelry, silver, gold, and art. They filled Lauer Ward's car up and sped off less than thirty minutes after killing him. The couple then drove straight across the state line out of Nebraska.

With all of the gruesome murder scenes being discovered in this short time period, Nebraska police departments, specifically Lancaster County, were scrambling for answers. Upon the Wards' murder discovery, a community lock down was issued. Each home was searched for possible leads and information. Their big break, however, was soon to come.

Having fled to Wyoming, the couple knew that they needed a new car. Ward's car drew too much attention and was wanted by law enforcement. The last murder of the killing spree was soon to take place. Traveling salesmen Merle Collison was asleep in his Buick on the side of the road. The couple drove by and realized their opportunity. Upon awakening Collison, Starkweather delivered a single shotgun blast to Collison's head. They had secured their new vehicle.

Popular culture focuses on this murder precisely for the actions of Caril Fugate. Caril reportedly performed a *coup-de-grace*. As Starkweather had an issue with his shotgun, Fugate supposedly delivered the fatal wound. While Fugate denies this, many believe this to be true. Charles Starkweather described her as "the most trigger happy person" he knew.

To Starkweather's luck, the salesmen's car that he had stolen had a unique push-pedal emergency brake system. He was completely unfamiliar with how to operate it. The car stalled repeatedly as the couple was making their getaway. A passing motorist stopped to offer assistance to the couple. He was immediately threatened with his life by Starkweather and his shotgun. A brief struggle ensued.

During the struggle, a deputy sheriff passed by the scene. As the sheriff exited his vehicle, Caril Fugate ran to the sheriff exclaiming, "It's Starkweather! He's going to kill me!" Starkweather jumped in the car and sped away. With officers in close pursuit, speeds in the chase exceeded 100 miles per hour. With gun blasts raining down on Starkweather's car, a stray bullet shattered the glass next to him causing lacerations. It was at this time that Charles Starkweather gave himself up.

"He thought he was bleeding to death. That's why he stopped. That's the kind of yellow son of a bitch he is," said Sheriff Earl Heflin.

Starkweather and Fugate were extradited back to Nebraska in late January 1958. Initially, he claimed that Fugate had no participation in the murders. After much questioning, his story changed numerous times. He would eventually agree that she was a willing participant.

Fugate claimed that she was held against her will. She claimed that her families lives were being threatened, and she had no idea that they were already dead. The judge firmly believed that she was an active participant. He felt that she had ample opportunity to escape. Caril Fugate was charged with murder and received a life sentence on November 21, 1958. She served 17 ½ years and was paroled. Caril moved to Michigan and changed her name. She married in 2007 and, despite a serious automobile accident that killed her husband and left her seriously injured, is still alive today. She has done only one major radio interview about the killing spree. She has stayed mute on the subject in her years after prison.

Charles Starkweather was found guilty of murder and given the death penalty. He was executed by way of the electric chair at 12:04 a.m. on June 25, 1959 at Nebraska State Penitentiary.

For just under two months, the crimes committed by Charles Starkweather and Caril Fugate can only be described as disturbing. Such senseless killing at the hands of a strange couple in the early years of their life. Many describe Starkweather as a stray dog. He is imaged this way as the animal that gets a taste of blood that can't seem to let it go. For Charles Starkweather and Caril Fugate, they got a taste of blood and strived to kill all that they could. If not for that sheriff driving by their struggle on the highway, the true numbers of this spree could have been exponentially higher. To anyone familiar with the case, Charles Starkweather got exactly what he deserved.

The Wolf Family Massacre

Carina David

97

The Wolf family massacre

The tale of the murders of Jacob Wolf, his wife and five children, and their hired help who was also a relative by marriage to the family is chilling, to say the least. The only survivor of this horrible crime was little baby Emma who was eight months old at the time of the murder.

There are many different theories out there today about what actually happened. Many people believe different things due to the complex case that it was. Henry Layer, a resident on a neighboring farm of the Wold family and was accused of the murder and sentenced to prison. Things got a bit complicated when he went on to sign 3 affidavits, the first where he admitted his guilt, and the last two when he was pleading his innocence. This caused a lot of tension at that time, and even now, and caused a lot of questions to come up.

It all started just a little while after the murder, two days to be exact. John Kraft and his wife drove into the yard of the Wolf farm. They hooted, and everything was deathly quiet, except they could hear the faint cry of a baby inside the Wolf family home. They hooted once again, and the baby gave a strong cry.

Nobody came out so Mr. Kraft and his wife went inside to investigate. As they walked into the kitchen, they saw no bodies but traces of blood that led to the cellar trap door. When they looked in, that is when they saw the bodies of Mrs. Wolf, three of her daughters and the body of Jakob Hofer, the hired help.

They later came upon the bodies of Mr. Wolf and his two oldest daughters which were covered in hay in the shed. John Kraft tried to phone someone for help but then he noticed the lines had been cut. They then took baby Emma who was worn out from hunger, crying and cold, back to their home to take care of her there. Reports say that she was very weak at that time. They phoned the police and that's when the investigation began. It was just two weeks after the crime when police took Henry Layer into custody and accused him of the murder of the Wolf family, eight victims in total.

In his first signed affidavit, his confession, he said that he left his home and went to see Mr. Wolf about an issue they had been having with Mr. Wolf's dogs. Apparently, the dog had bitten one of his cows and he wanted Mr. Wolf to come look at the cow to assess the damage done. He said that he walked into the house, into the kitchen where Mr. Wolf, his wife, his five children and their hired hand, Jakob Hofer were sitting.

Apparently, Mr. Wolf had told Layer to go away and that when Layer had refused to leave and tried to reason with him, that Mr. Wolf went to get his double-barrelled shotgun out of the front room. According to Layer, there was a struggle and then two shots were fired in a quick succession of one another. If this was the case, these were the two shots that killed Mrs. Wolf and the hired hand, Jakob Hofer. Mrs. Beata Wolf was thirty-five years of age. She was shot in the back at close range. Jacob was shot through the back of his neck, and the bullet severed his jugular vein.

Layer then managed to get the gun away from Mr. Wolf and went to the front room and then took more shotgun shells from where he saw Wolf take the first two shotgun shells from, and reloaded the gun and started shooting the rest of the family. He said he cannot remember who he shot first but he thinks that he started by shooting Mr. Wolf. He says that Mr. Wolf had started running towards the cowshed when he shot him the first time. There were two shots fired again. One at a long distance which went in his back, and the other so close that it ripped three of his ribs away from his spine.

Layer then claims that he then went into the cowshed and found two of Wolf's daughters, Maria and Edna, who were aged 9 and 7, hiding in the corner and that he shot them where they stood. Maria was shot in the back of the head behind her left ear. Edna was also shot in the back of her head at close range.

Apparently, Layer saw the little girls running from the house to the cow shed which is why he went there to kill them. Investigators confirm this as the window in their parents' room which is where they probably were folding clothes, was open wide enough for them to get through. There was also footprint evidence under the window.

Little Liddia who was about five years old at the time, was shot at the back of her left ear and had a second blow to her head with a hatchet. And the youngest victim, little Martha who was three years old was the only one who did not sustain wounds from a shotgun, instead, she died from a blow with the broad side of the hatchet blade to her head.

He went on to cover the bodies of the girls with hay and then placed Wolf on top of the girls and covered him with his coat and with more Hay. He then opened the trap door that lead from the kitchen to the basement and then he threw the rest of the bodies into the basement and then put down the trap door.

When asked why he did not kill baby Emma, he said it was because she was sleeping at the time of the incident and he did not go into that room. He pulled out the telephone wires and he left the house and closed the doors.

He said he picked up all the empty shells and carried them with him. He broke the gun and threw the broken gun and the shells into the slough. He said that he then went to his house which was approximately two miles away. He said he believed he got home about three hours after he had first gone to the Wolfs' farm.

He then added, at the end, as if it was an afterthought that when he finished shooting in the cowshed, he threw three or four empty shells into the hayloft through an open door. This was signed May 13, 1920, not even three weeks after the massacre.

The funeral

The funeral for the murdered family was held in Turtle Lake. There were over 2 500 people in attendance, even though turtle lake only had a total population of 395. People who had heard about the story came from far and wide. This type of crime was unheard of at that time, and up until this day, it remains one of the most horrendous mysteries and horrible murders of time.

At that time there was nobody in custody for the murder of the Wolf family and Jakob Hofer yet, but many had suspicions as to who the culprit might be. There are some reports that accused Henry of being the murder at the time. They say that Henry Layer opened the caskets and gazed at the faces of the dead family members. But, this was actually the norm back then. Everyone was expecting an open-casket funeral.

There were at least two people who helped prepare the bodies for the funeral as they knew that people would see them, so they wanted to make them look as decent and as respectable as possible. The bodies were so badly mutilated that it even caused one of the women who were helping to clean up the bodies faint. Everyone looked at the mutilated faces of the dead family, including Layer. The women held back shrieks and the men held back their tears. This was not a reason to suspect him at the time, although, after being accused of the murder, people did find it very scary that if he did kill them, he managed to look at all of their bodies after the time. This would have had to be a very sick person.

A separate service was held for Jakob Hofer, who was murdered along with the family. It was held at the farm home of his parents, Bernhardt and Caroline Hofer. He was buried with Jacob and Beata Wolf, as well as their five children at the Turtle Lake Cemetery.

Another theory.

Because of all the questions that came up and the fact that so many people were killed without anyone hearing anything lead to many people making up their own theories.

Rumor at the time was that Mr. Wolf was having sexual relations with one of Layer's daughters. There was never ever evidence about this matter but that would have been the perfect motive.

Layer said that he entered the house to talk to Wolf which was also strange because it is well documented that Wolf had two very good sheepdogs which would have alerted him that there was someone at the farm gate. He would have then gone outside to see who it was. This was the custom in that day. No man would just walk into the home of another.

Reports from neighbors also show that the incident of the dogs biting Layer's cattle was not new and it had been ongoing for six months. Neighbors said that Layer and Wolf were not on talking terms. Wolf would not have let Layer into his house, into the kitchen where his wife and children were sitting if these were indeed the circumstances.

Layer says that he threw everybody into the cellar but as shown from pictures of the scene there was one puddle of blood in the kitchen. Also, the body of Jakob Hofer, the hired helper, was the only one that was on the floor right in front of the ladder, so he was the only one that would have been thrown down.

One of the theories is that the murders were committed during breakfast and not at noon. Also that Mrs. Wolf and her three daughters were not killed in the kitchen, but instead in the cellar where they might have been hiding, or made to go by the attackers.

Investigators found the body of Mrs. Wolf behind the ladder and contrary to the statement by Layer; the investigators had originally believed that Mrs. Wolf was indeed shot in the basement which would have made more sense because of where her body was found.

They then theorize that Hofer was probably coming into the kitchen in the morning, and was shot from behind. They then think that the oldest daughters had tried to run away after hearing the events in the kitchen, which is why they fled from the house and into the cow shed and they hid behind the haystack, which is where they were shot.

What was also suspicious was the fact that in his first statement he said that he threw the broken gun and all the shells in the slough, but afterwards he said that he had thrown more shells through an open door. They all landed in a chicken nest, neatly against each other.

The fact that he had said that in an afterthought was suspicious to some. Also the fact that he was the one that found them and reported them made people wonder that if he was the murderer, would he have not hid them instead of reporting it to the investigators. The fact that the shotgun shells were lying there led people to believe that there were two people involved in the massacre and that someone was waiting there for Bertha and Jacob to come from the fields on hearing the gunshots, and then killing them.

What was also questionable about his first statement was the fact that he said the first two shots that went off by accident were the ones to kill Mrs. Wolf and Jacob, although it is highly unlikely to have two accident shots go off and shoot two people. One was shot in the neck and the other behind the ear. There is no saying what distance they stood at and where they were positioned. It is plausible but unlikely.

According to Layer, the shotgun belonged to Mr. Wolf. The shotgun was found by one of the numerous neighbors that had gone to the farm the day after the murder had been reported. Nobody could verify that the shotgun did indeed belong to Wolf. His friends and relatives also did not recognize the gun.

The oldest daughter and Hofer had gloves on when they were killed, which were still on their hands when their bodies were found. This might show that they were working in the field before they were murdered.

Circumstances of the first confession.

On August 10th, Layer signed another affidavit in which he described the interrogation. He said that a few days after the funeral, four men came to his house and told him to go with them to talk about the killing.

While on their way to Washburn, they stopped and captured another man who Layer thought was an escaped convict from the prison. They put both of them in prison. The convict told Layer that he had a way to escape but Layer refused to go along with any of his plans. They saw each other often and the convict would always ask Layer why he was in prison. His reply was always the same – for no reason.

On May 12th, he went to the Sheriff's office and was questioned. This was no normal interview. Layer claims that he was continuously shown pictures of the murder scene. They carried on the interview until the early hours of the morning.

Layer claims that he was threatened. He was told that there was a mob outside waiting for him as they wanted to take the course of justice upon themselves. Apparently, he was told that the only way that he would ever survive was to confess to the crime and go to jail.

He said that they swore at him and took his chair away and made him stand to the point that he got dizzy. He kept saying he was innocent even through all of this. After that, one of the men in the room hit hum on the side of his head, took him by the hair and pulled him around the room.

Layer claims that this man then sat across the table from him and told him exactly how the murder happened, what he was to say, and then he got up, shook a club in his face and then threatened him by saying that if he did not say that, he would beat him to death.

Layer then gave up. He was crying and then said that he would do as they wished. They then called someone in to write down the confession.

More questions

An affidavit signed by a prison barber at the time confirmed the statements in the second affidavit of Layer.

When Henry Layer arrived at the State Penitentiary in Bismarck, North Dakota, that Myrle Cook had just started acting as a barber there. He said that he shaved Henry Layer and gave him a haircut. He said that when he started working on him, he saw that Layer was badly beaten up and that both sides of his face and the top of his head were swollen and it was obvious that he had been beaten by someone.

He asked Layer what had happened. In reply, Layer told him that he was beaten by the man who had charge of him before he was brought to the institution. He apparently broke down and cried very much and kept on saying that he was innocent.

Dr. C. E. Stackhouse said under oath that he had examined Layer and found him to be in a "normal physical condition". He said that there were two areas of ecchymosis on his face, one over each cheek bone and about the size of a silver dollar but that there was no swelling.

Both these affidavits from these persons show that there must have been some sort of incident. But one describes it as not such a big deal, whereas the other said that Layer had been badly beaten and that there was swelling. Will we ever know the truth?

An affidavit signed by Layer's brother-in-law, William Brokofsky was also in support of Layer's petition for a change of plea. William and Henry's wife, Lydia, went to the State Penitentiary of Bismarck, North Dakota to go see Henry on the first Sunday after he was committed. They asked to see and talk to him but they were refused. They were told that Henry was not in a condition to be seen.

A short while after, they went again to see him. This time they got to see and talk to Henry. This was the first time that William had a chance to talk to him since his confinement and Henry kept on telling him he was innocent. He had also told him under which circumstances he had to admit to the crime.

Lydia Layer also signed an affidavit dated December 20, 1920, which said that she and Henry were married and they were well acquainted with the Wold family. The said that she was at home all day on the 22nd of April, and did the usual work which was hers to do.

She said that she knew of her husband's whereabouts and that Henry was working in the fields that day and that he never left the farm during any part of the day. She said that at noon, at the usual hour, Henry came home and ate and then returned to work which was the usual.

Physical evidence – or the lack thereof

There was no physical evidence that could connect Layer to the murders. The case was wrapped up quickly because people were terrified and others wanted the case to be closed quickly.

More about the accused

Henry Layer, born Heinrich C. Layer was born on the 12 of November 1884 is Eigenfeld, South Russia. HE moved to the country in 1886. Lydia was his second wife. His first wife was Mathilda Miller. They had two children who went by the names of Elizabeth Katherina and Edward. The couple was divorced in March 1911 and the children stayed with their mother.

He went on to marry Lydia Brokofsky Hinzman in January 1912. He was sentenced to life in prison on May 13th, 1920. He and his wife were divorced on December 21, 1922. It is believed that they were divorced so that Layer could free his wife from any legal obligations towards him and that she could move on. Layer then died in hospital on March 21, 1925, after having a blood clot go through his heart after receiving an appendectomy. His wife then remarried only after his death, in November 1925.

Authorities said that Layer was a model prisoner and that he had acted as the head man in the laundry. The obituary stated that he was buried in a local cemetery but up until this day, it is not known exactly where he was buried.

Who was Jakob Hofer?

Jakob was the son of Bernhardt Hofer, who is a brother to Emanuel Whober, who married the sister of Beata Wolf, Christina Bossert. He was only thirteen years old at the time of the incident. He is often referred to as the hired help because Mr. Jakob Wolf had hired him to help him with the spring plantation after a boy who was supposed to help him had to decline. He was in fact family.

What happened to little baby Emma?

The incident happened when baby Emma was just eight months old. She was found just in time because she was so weak already from all the crying, the cold, and going without food or anything to drink. Even though her life was spared, one can just think what kind of an impact that would have had on the rest of her life.

Emma was in attendance at the funeral of her family at that very young age. She lived with her mother's sister and her husband but they passed away in the 1930's. After that, she was put into the guardianship of a couple who lived near her hometown, Turtle Lake. She later went on to study teaching.

Emma carried on to live her entire life in the Turtle Lake area. She was married in 1940 to a gentleman named Clarence Hanson. They had three children. Emma lived a happy life and she died on the 16th of October, 2003 at the advanced age of 84.

More tragedy struck

After her husband had gone to prison and they divorced, 5 of the six Layer children went to an orphanage in Minnesota, and only the youngest that was a year old at that stage had stayed with his mother. One of their children, Berthold Layer was killed at age 6. While at the orphanage the children were playing at one of the farm gates.

According to the Fairmont Sentinel, little Berthold had been told to stay away from the wagon that was coming in with sugar beets on the back. All of a sudden the driver, F.C, Fuller, felt the back of the wagon lift up.

Berthold must have fallen underneath it and it drove over him. His skull had cracked at its' base and his death was said to be instant. His siblings, two brothers, and one sister, who had seen what happened. The youngest who was 4 at the time, Edwin, could not understand it and just cried while he tried to console his siblings, Blanche and his brothers Alvin and Emil.

A twist to the tale

In mid-November 1920, new evidence was found on the Wolf farm. John Hofer and his wife and four children were now renting the land. While playing outside, two of the young children made a thrilling discovery. In some bushes not too far from the house, wrapped in an oil tablecloth, were two homemade cloth masks, a woman's worn dusting cap, and a shotgun shell.

The one mask was large and had holes for the eyes and mouth. Another, smaller mask only had holes for the eyes. The empty shotgun shell was identical to the one found at the scene of the crime. One of the masks and the dusting cap had blood on them.

It is believed that this evidence was planted because hundreds of neighbors came to comb over the farm to look for evidence and investigators are sure they would have found it. But it was planted, or just missed; it is believed that these objects were related to the murder. It is believed that these objects could belong to a man and a woman. Are they the murderers? Or were they involved in the murders?

Conclusion

There are certainly some unanswered questions about this case. Many people were hurt by these events. The Wolf family, the Layer family, the Hofer family, and all the people that knew and loved them. It had quite an impact on all the children at that time, as we can only imagine. The murder tore families apart and it still causes confusion to this day. Will we ever know the answers to these questions? Will justice ever be served? Maybe it already has been, and perhaps, it never will be.

THE JUST DO IT KILLER

SARAH THOMPSON

McCamey, Texas. A town of less than two thousand people, out in the scorching Texas desert, where downtown is a stretch of black road with marginally more buildings on either side. McCamey is the type of town that lies, more or less, entirely forgotten by the rest of the United States, down in the deep heat of Texas. It was in McCamey, in 1940, that Gary Mark Gilmore was born. Gilmore would have, perhaps, gone one to live and die a completely unnoticed life if circumstances had been different. As it stands, Gary Mark Gilmore would gain fame through his life for being the first person sentenced to death in the United States in nearly ten years for the crimes that he committed.

On December 4th, in 1940, Frank and Bessie Gilmore became the parents of their second son, Gary Mark Gilmore. Frank and Bessie were married on a whim, and Frank was said to have other wives and families that he otherwise ignored. Bessie was a Mormon from Provo, Utah, but she had been outcast by her community. Bessie and Frank met and married in California, but the both of them eventually moved to McCamey, Texas, where Gary Mark had been born. Gilmore would have three brothers: Frank Jr., Gaylen and Mikal Gilmore. It was in McCamey that Frank and Bessie were living with their first son Frank Jr., and existing under the false name of "Coffman" in order to escape detection from law enforcement. When he was born, Gary Mark Gilmore had been given the name Faye Robert Coffman - Faye, named after Frank Gilmore Sr.'s mother, Fay.

However, the name Faye Robert didn't stick. His mother, Bessie, decided to change it to Gary Mark Gilmore after they left Texas. Moving wasn't uncommon for the Gilmore family. Gary spent most of his childhood moving from city to city throughout most of the Western United States, along with this three brothers and his parents.

Frank Gilmore supported the family during this time with the sale of fraudulent magazine subscriptions. Gary's relationship with his father was rocky, as was the rest of the family's relationship with Frank Gilmore, Sr. He was described as a man with a quick temper, and who was easily angered. He was also a strict father, and one to dole out corporal punishment when and if he saw fit. Frank often did not need a reason to beat his sons, and would routinely whip them with a razor strop, belt or whip.

Frank Gilmore, Sr. did not only take out his anger and violence on his sons. Though this was less frequent, he would also take to beating Bessie. The relationship between Frank and Bessie was also volatile. Gary grew up in a household in which his parents would often take to screaming at one another, and verbally abusing one another with insults and digs at each other's religions. Bessie would even threatened to kill Frank Sr. some nights. The two parental figures of the household were constantly at one another's throats, and it was the source of a lot of distress and frustration and turmoil within the Gilmore family.

Exposure to violence between his mother and father and the crimes of his father did nothing for Gary's disposition. While his other brothers seemed to escape the thrall of their household unscathed, Gary wasn't so lucky. There's no telling what a calmer household would have done for Gary, and if his rocky home life was the root cause for the crimes he would commit and the path he would soon begin to take in life.

Despite the Gilmore family's nomadic lifestyle for the greater part of Gary's children, they finally settled down in Portland, Oregon in the year 1952. Gary was twelve at the time, and like most twelve year olds, he was starting to stretch his legs and discover some semblance of independence and self-identity. During his adolescence, Gary was incredibly intelligent. He tested an IQ score of 133, and throughout his schooling career he tested and scored well on both aptitude and achievement tests. Gary even showed an incredible ability for artistic talent. He was on the entirely right track to being a successful student and graduating from school.

Unfortunately, Gary did not continue down this path. He was in the ninth grade when he decided to drop out of high school. It was then that Gary became caught up in petty crimes, and took to anti-social behaviors. After he dropped out of high school, Gary ran away from home with a friend. They traveled from Oregon all the way down to Texas. There they stayed for several months before finally returning back to Portland. It was at 14 that he finally managed to succumb to his first arrest. He had started a car theft ring with some friends. Rather than put him in jail, law enforcement released him back to his father and all Gary received from police was a slap on the wrist and a warning to keep in line.

Gary didn't take either the warning or the gift seriously. It wasn't any more than two weeks later when Gary found himself back in court on yet another charge for car theft. At this point, the court sent Gary to the MacLaren Reform School for Boys. The MacLaren Reform School was a correctional facility located in Woodburn, Oregon. The boys residing in MacLaren were anywhere from age 13 to 25, and had committed and range of crimes. In retrospect, due to Gary's immense intelligence and his own willful nature, it might have been the fact that he was sent to MacLaren that had redoubled his affinity for crime, or at least his unwillingness to stop.

Gary was released the next year from MacLaren, but he didn't stay out for long. For the next several years, Gary would be in and out of prison for various crimes. In 1960, at 20 years old, Gary was convicted of another car theft. This time, he was sentenced to time in the Oregon State Correctional Institute. He served a minimal amount of time there, and was even released later in the year. It was around this time in 1961, that Gary's father, Frank Gilmore Sr., was diagnosed with lung cancer. It was terminal. Gary's tumultuous relationship with his father was coming to an end.

In 1962, Gary was once more arrested. This time, the crime was much more severe than stealing a car. He was charged with armed robbery and assault, and was sentenced to Oregon State Penitentiary. It was during this stint in prison that Frank Gilmore Sr. passed away from lung cancer. Gary was in prison at the time and was unable to say goodbye, or even receive the news directly from his family. One of the guards that the Oregon State Penitentiary gave Gary the news about his father's passing.

Gary's relationship with his father had never been good. He grew up in a household where his father and mother were always at odds, with him and his brother's caught in the middle. Frank Gilmore, Sr. was brutal, violent and strict on his sons. He went beyond disciplining them when he raised his belt or whip against Gary and his brothers. Mikal had even once described their father as a "cruel and unreasonable man". And yet, despite all of that - despite the years spent moving around at the whim of his con man father, and despite the years spent at the end of a leather strop and watching his father beat his mother, Gary Gilmore was distraught over the old man's death. When he was given the news of Frank Sr.'s passing, Gary tried to end his life by slitting his wrists.

The suicide attempt was unsuccessful, and Gary Gilmore remained alive. He was eventually released back into suicide. For two years, Gary either stayed out of trouble or managed not to get caught. And yet, in 1964, Gary was once more returned to prison - on the charges of armed robbery and assault, once more. This time, Gary was sentenced to fifteen years in prison for his habitual offenses. A prison psychiatrist finally diagnosed Gary with antisocial personality disorder as well as something called intermittent psychotic decompensation. Psychotic decompensation is a term that describes the rapid deterioration of someone's mental health that they had been, up until then, been otherwise maintaining. This, along with Gary's personality disorder characterized by his disregard and often violation of other people's rights and autonomy, make him a perfect package for crime.

By the time he was 30, Gary Gilmore had spent the greater part of his adult life in and out of prison. The intelligence that had heard him such high marks and a promising future when he was a boy didn't disappear over the years. In fact, Gary used much of his time in prison to write poetry and make artwork. It was these talents that initially won Gary conditional release to a halfway house in Eugene, Oregon. In 1972, he was granted permission to live weekdays at the halfway house under the condition that he stay out of trouble and take art classes at the local community college. However, in line with Gary's usual behavior, he ended up never registering for classes at the community college. Within a month of his initial conditional release, Gary Gilmore couldn't resist the siren call of crime, and was once more arrested and convicted on the charge of armed robbery.

Gary Gilmore's behavior in prison turned from quiet poetry crafting to violence, and he was eventually transferred to a maximum-security federal prison in Marion, Illinois. He was transferred there in 1975. Now 35, it was looking like Gary Gilmore would be spending many more years of is still short life in prison. While he was serving his time in Marion, Gary began writing letters with his cousin, Brenda Nicol. Perhaps it was through Gary's particular intelligence that he manipulated her into believing he deserved a second change, or maybe it was Brenda's own idea. All the same, in 1976, Gary was once more given conditional release into the care of his cousin, Brand. He would live with her in Provo, Utah, under the condition that he stay out of trouble. Brenda would help him look for work and aid in his reform, offering Gary a support system that he had not had previously.

Gary began working at a shoe repair store owned by his uncle, Vern Damico. He also worked, briefly, for an insulation company. This rehabilitation seemed to be on the up and up, and Gary's life was being steered clear of all his previous habits. Unfortunately, Gary wasn't able to keep away from his old ways for long. Soon after his foray into a new life, Gary was back into his old habits of drinking, stealing and fighting. He got into a relationship with a 19 year old woman by the name of Nicole Baker. Nicole was both a window and a divorcee and she had two young children at the time that she and Gary got together. Their relationship was casual at first, but it didn't take long for things between Gary and Nicole to become both intense and strained. Perhaps it was from his own parent's relationship that Gary had learned how to interact with others in a romantic sense - that is, he didn't learn very well at all.

Gary soon began imitate his father. He became controlling with Nicole, and threatening. Their relationship was strained both from Gary's violent behavior, as well as pressure from Nicole's family for her to leave him. Gary was having trouble adjusting to life outside of prison, after spending nearly half of his life, and almost all of his adult life, behind bars. His relationship with Nicole was just a precursor to Gary's inevitable inability to reform himself and stay the straight and narrow path.

It all came to a head on July 19th, 1976. Gary Gilmore stopped at a gas station in Orem, Utah. He had been travelling at the time with April, Nicole Baker's younger sister. During this time, Gary and Nicole were still off-again on-again, in an unstable and volatile relationship. It was around 10:30 in the evening that Gary stopped and told April that he needed to make a phone call. He left April in the car and entered the gas station. It was there that he robbed the gas station attendant, Max Jensen, at gunpoint, continuing his affinity for armed robbery. This time, however, Gary took it another step. After Gary had instructed Jensen to give him the money box, he forced him into the bathroom and had him lay down on the floor. Max Jensen obeyed all of Gary's demands, but his obedience was for naught. According to Gary's confession of the crime, he held his gun against Jensen's head and said,

"This one is for me," before firing the gun once. He then stated, "For Nicole", before firing the gun a second time, shooting Jensen twice and then leaving him, dead and bleeding, on the bathroom floor of the gas station.

Leaving Orem behind, Gary traveled back to Provo with April and spent the night in a motel nearby where he left his truck in a service garage to be repaired. The evening after his armed robbery and murder in Orem, Gary robbed a hotel manager by the name of Ben Bushnell, who lived on the property with his family. Much like the victim before him, Ben Bushnell complied with every one of Gary's demands. An eyewitness, motel guest Peter Arroyo, would later describe Gary ordering Bushnell to lie on the floor. Much like Jensen, Bushnell was shot and killed. When he tried to dispose of his weapon that he used in both robberies and murders, Gary managed to accidentally shoot himself in his right hand. Had he not, he might have managed to get away with both killings and continue on to commit more escalated violence. As it were, his bleeding hand alerted the garage mechanic, Michael Simpson, who had seen Gary trying to hide the gun in the nearby bushes.

Michael Simpson wrote down Gary's license plate number after hearing about a shooting at a nearby motel on a police scanner. He called the police and alerted them of the goings on, of Gary's wounded hand and of his disposing of the gun in the bushes by the mechanic garage. Meanwhile, Gary had called his cousin for support, but she was unsympathetic to his plight. She called the police as well, and Gary was taken into custody after law enforcement found him at the edge of town not long after the incident.

Gary Mark Gilmore isn't the most prolific killer in history, or even of his time. He probably wouldn't even be classified as a serial killer, or even a spree killer. It's Gary's particular circumstances that make him so famous, however. It was the same year that Gary Mark Gilmore was arrested for two counts of murder that the U.S Supreme Court upheld a series of new death penalty statutes in the court decision of Gregg v. Georgia. Before that, death penalty statutes had been deemed "cruel and unusual punishment", and therefore deemed unconstitutional. It wasn't until the 1976 Supreme Court decision that the death penalty was reinstated. Perhaps, if this ruling had not occurred, Gary Mark Gilmore would have rotted away in life in prison as many others had before him during the time where the death penalty was not in effect. Gary Mark Gilmore was charged with both the murders of Jensen and Bushnell, though only Bushnell's murder actually went to trial, due to a lack of evidence and eyewitnesses to Jensen's murder—even though Gary admitted to both.

He was held in custody until October 5th, 1976. It was on that day that Gary Mark Gilmore's trail began in Provo. It lasted only two days. Unhappy with his lawyers' lack of cross-examination and lack of their own witnesses for his defense, Gary persuaded the judge to let him take the stand in his own defense. He claimed dissociation and lack of control, and tried to make a case of insanity. His own attorney's called four separate psychiatrists to shoot down this attempt of claiming insanity, showing that Gary had full control and awareness of what he was doing during the crimes. Not even his antisocial personality disorder was enough for him to actually meet the legal definition of insanity. Despite his intelligence and his skilled manipulation tactics, Gary was not able to present a defense for himself. It seemed that he knew when he was beat.

On October 7, 1976, after two days of trial, the jury returned a guilty verdict. They also agreed on the death penalty, due to circumstances surrounding Gary's crimes. This would be the first execution in the United States in ten years, and the first execution that would happen after the Supreme Court decision to allow the death penalty once more.

Gary's mother, Bessie, attempted to sue to for a stay of execution, despite the fact that Gary himself chose not to pursue habeas corpus.

In a unanimous decision, the U.S Supreme Court refused to even hear Bessie's claim, and her son was slated to be executed. A death penalty sentence in modern times includes lethal injection, as it has been proven to be the most humane way of sentencing a criminal to death, unlike the methods of the past such as hanging or the electric chair. During Utah in 1976, however, the only methods available for executions were hanging, or a firing squad. Gary Mark Gilmore had already accepted his fate as the first man to be executed in the United States in almost ten years. To Gary, a hanging had room for error. He told the court, "I prefer to be shot," and chose the firing squad. Thus, his execution was set for 8 am on November 15th.

Despite having accepted his fate, Gary ended up actually receiving a few stays of execution, though he did not seek them out and explicitly did not want them. It was at the hands of the American Civil Liberties Union (ACLU) and his attorneys that drew out his already chosen execution. When his lawyers tried to call of an appeal on his case, Gary opted instead to fire them. He was ready to face his death, and he saw no reason to draw it out any longer. It was this refusal of appeal that drew the ACLU's attention. The ACLU made efforts, hand in hand with the National Association for the Advancement of Colored People to turn over Gary's execution. However, it wasn't entirely for Gary's benefit. They were using Gary's case to benefit the prisoners who were standing on death row throughout the United States, all of whom were now in danger of facing execution now that the Supreme Court had reinstated the death penalty.

Gary's execution got tied up in legalities. He was ready for it to all be over. In November 1976, while Gary was taking part in a Board of Pardons hearing, Gary said this of all the legal attempts to spare his life: "It's been sanctioned by the courts that I die and I accept that." The dragged out legal battle between the courts and the ACLU put off Gary's execution for months, and in the interim Gary attempted suicide twice. His first attempted occurred on November 16th when his first stay of execution was announced. Nicole Barrett visited Gary in prison, despite her having broken off their relationship. They kissed and held one another during Nicole's visit, and the reason for it became clear. Nicole had snuck in sleeping pills. After she had left, Gary swallowed the overdose of pills—while at the same time, miles away in her own home, Nicole Barrett had done the same, the both of them attempting suicide. Gary had not taken enough sleeping pills for the dosage to be fatal. Nicole took a larger dosage of sleeping pills, which resulted in her slipping into a coma for several days. Gary was not finished with attempting to end his life. With or without Nicole, Gary attempted suicide again one month later to the exact day in December. When that didn't work, he took up a hunger strike.

Finally, Gary was given a date for execution: January 17th, 1977. On the night before his execution, Gary requested that he be allowed to have an all-night gathering that consisted of his friends and family. He was granted the request, and spent his last evening surrounded by the people in his life that could be considered his loved ones. Gary's last meal consisted of potatoes and steak to eat, and milk and coffee to drink. For whatever reason, Gary didn't touch his steak and potatoes. The last thing that he had was the milk and the coffee. The next morning, on January 17th, Gary's last stay of execution was overturned at 7:30 AM, and Gary was finally allowed to go through with his execution as he had wanted so many months previously.

At 8:07 AM, Gary was taken behind the prison to an abandoned cannery. He was placed and secured into a chair with a wall of sandbags behind him for the purpose of absorbing the bullets. In tradition of firing squad, five local police were placed behind a cloth with only a small hole for them to put through the barrel of their rifles, aimed directly at his body from 20 feet away. In Utah tradition, the firing squad consists of four men with live rounds and one man with a blank round. This is done, ostensibly, so that the men comprised of the firing squad will never know which one of them fired the killing shot.

When he was asked for any last words, all Gary Mark Gilmore had to say was this: "Let's do it!" A black hood was placed on his head, and the five gunmen were allowed to fire a single bullet into the body of the first man to undergo execution in the United States in almost ten years. Gary's youngest brother, Mikal Gilmore, was allowed to inspect the clothes worn by his brother after his execution. Allegedly, there were five holes left in the clothes, not four. He noted this in his memoir, 'Shot in the Heart', and mused that Utah wanted to take no chances on leaving his brother alive. Mikal's memoir goes in depth into his relationship with Gary, as well as the strained relationship he had with his family, as well as the aftermath of his own brother's execution at the hands of the state of Utah.

Before his death, Gary had requested that his organs be donated to those in need of transplant. Because of his death by firing squad, it can be presumed that some of his internal organs were useless, now riddled with bullet holes - mainly, his heart, where a piece of black cloth had been pinned as a target for the firing squad. Strangely enough, though, two people were able to receive corneal transplants, courtesy of now famed murderer Gary Mark Gilmore. After his autopsy, Gary's body was cremated. In a grandiose decision by his family, Gary's ashes were then scattered from an airplane over Spanish Fork, Utah.

Gary Mark Gilmore is notorious, perhaps not for his crimes, but for when his crimes occurred. He would have otherwise rotted away in prison, unknown but for the people whose lives he had touched, no matter how horrid and terrible that touch may be. It was by virtue of the place and time that he had committed his crimes that gained Gary Mark Gilmore his fame of being the first man executed in the United States since the death penalty had been reinstated. It is more than just those who were involved in his case and legal battles that remember his name. Gary Mark Gilmore is now known for his own battle for execution. He is remembered in both the minds of those involved, as well as the legal histories of the United States.

The Texarkana Moonlight Murders

IRIS HULSE

Texarkana has always been an unusual place. On the east, you have Texarkana, Arkansas, a small town by any other measurement, yet home to the largest population in Miller County. To the west lies Texarkana, Texas, located in rural Bowie County and lucky enough to have its very own Wal-Mart. Together these twin cities make up what is simply referred to as "Texarkana."

Texarkana is a dusty town, built on a foundation of competing railroads and a Mexican border dispute in the 1800s. The town laid low for the next several years, sending off its sons to fight World War I and then II, and welcoming them back home for better or for worse. But no one in Texarkana was prepared for the national attention that came in the spring of 1946. On February 22nd, 1946, a masked serial killer, dubbed the "Phantom Killer" by the *Texarkana Gazette*'s Calvin Sutton, began terrorizing young couples on the town's secluded country roads.

Today, if you search the Internet for information on Texarkana and its morbid history, you will likely be redirected to pages on *The Town That Dreaded Sundown* and its Arkansan producer, Charles B. Pierce. In 1977, decades after the last murders, this film joined the ranks of *Halloween* and *The Texas Chainsaw Massacre* as one of Hollywood's classic horrors, featuring countless local residents as set extras. While the film's accuracy is something to be questioned, it remains a key piece of the town's identity. Visitors can even catch a screening every Halloween at Spring Lake Park, not far from where one of the infamous murders took place.

Texarkana may have embraced its celebrity status, but eighty years ago the town was paralyzed in fear. Within a single spring, five were dead and three were wounded. All in what had previously been a quiet, friendly community.

A Masked Attacker

Just before midnight, on February 22nd, 1946, Jimmy Hollis and Mary Jeanne Larey were finishing up their date in the backseat of

Hollis' father's car. Hollis, 24, and Larey, 19, had been dating for a while, but his parents expected the car (and the lovebirds) home by midnight. Throwing caution to the wind, they parked on a secluded dirt road, known as a lovers' lane, and proceeded to do what young couples will do.

The pair was soon startled by a flashlight, shining through the driver side window and blinding them to whoever stood outside. Hollis quickly composed himself and opened the door, thinking they were being interrupted by an ill-timed police patrol or a prank from some local kids, but they found themselves face-to-face with a masked man holding a gun.

Hollis continued to confront the intruder, telling him, "Fellow, you've got me mixed up with someone else. You got the wrong man." Hollis later said that the masked man muttered something like, "I don't want to kill you, so do what I say." Hollis attempted to calm the assailant, who forced the young man out of the vehicle and demanded Hollis remove his pants, gun pointed squarely at his face. Larey pleaded with Hollis to do as the man said, thinking he would not become violent if they did as he said. Instead the masked man overpowered Hollis, beating him over the head with the revolver. As Hollis lay limp on the cold ground, the attack continued until the sound of Hollis' skull cracking echoed throughout the clearing.

At this point Larey was hysterical with panic, thinking the loud crack of Hollis' broken skull was the sound of him being shot. She told the man they had no money or valuables, attempting to hand the man Hollis' wallet, but he only screamed, "Liar," at her and demanded her purse. Then the masked man told her to run toward the road. Larey ran as fast as she could, but the strange man pursued, continuing to scream, "Liar," at her as she ran.

The assailant eventually outpaced Larey, and forced her to the ground. Larey reported that the man did not rape her, but that assaulted her violent and used his gun to sexually molest her. Larey was afraid for her life, fighting against the weight of her attacker. She eventually managed to escape his grasp, rising up and telling him, "Go ahead and kill me." She then ran to a nearby house at 805 Blanton Street, where she managed to wake up the sleeping woners and pleaded for help. Shortly after, the Bowie County Sheriff, W.H. "Bill" Presley, arrived at what would be the first known Phantom Killer crime scene.

Hollis and Larey were lucky enough to survive this first attack, though they were left with plenty of physical and emotional scars to show for it. Hollis and Larey described their attacker as a tall man wearing a burlap sack with two slits cut for the eyes, though they could not agree on the man's race. Hollis believed the man was white, with tanned skin from working outdoors, while Larey insisted he was a black man because of his mannerisms and "curses." At this point, the attack was treated as a random attempted robbery, it was unknown the chaos that the Phantom Killer would bring in coming months.

The First Kill

In the early hours of March 24th, a truck driver spotted a young man asleep in an Oldsmobile parked on the side of the road. Concerned about the danger of passing traffic, the truck driver ran up to the window, hoping to wake the man and advise him of a better resting area. To the truck driver's horror, the young man was not asleep; he had been shot twice in the back of the head and sat dead in the driver's seat. In the Oldsmobile's backseat was a teenage girl wrapped in a bloody blanket, her body was completely lifeless. These young lovers were not as lucky as the Phantom Killer's first victims.

Richard Griffin, 29, was a retired Navy SeaBee on a double date with his girlfriend of six weeks, Polly Ann Moore, 17, when they pulled over on the highway to have some time alone. They had just finished up dinner with Griffin's sister and her boyfriend at a local café, and Griffin was in no rush to return his girlfriend to her parents' house. Unfortunately, they would never make it home.

Sometime that previous night, Griffin and Moore had pulled over onto the side of the road. It is believed they were approached similarly to the Phantom Killer's first victims, with a blinding flashlight and pointed gun. There was a heavy rainfall over Texarkana that night, so no one would have been out and about to see the killings take place.

Griffin was likely killed first, with two shots from a .32 Colt revolver to the back of his head. Moore, however, had been dragged from the vehicle and sexually assaulted on the cold, wet ground by their attacker. Blood and marks littered the dirt next to the vehicle. After this horror, Moore was also shot and killed by the Phantom Killer. The assailant pulled a blanket from the car's trunk and wrapped her in it before placing her body in the backseat of the Oldsmobile. Any fingerprints and footprints left behind by the killer that night was washed away by the storm.

Griffin's pockets were found empty and turned inside out, and Moore's purse remained at the scene but was emptied of any cash. With the only apparent motive being robbery, questions still remained as to why the crime was carried out so violently. The *Texarkana Gazette*, at the insistence of the Sheriff Bill Presley, made an announcement on March 27th asking residents to not spread rumors or anything else that they did not see with their own two eyes. Despite offering a cash reward, no solid tips ever made it to the police force.

Murder in the Park

Betty Jo Booker, 15, was a straight-A student who was adored by those around her. She worked with Jerry Atkins playing saxophone for a local band, The Rhythmaires, every Saturday night at the local VFW club. On April 14th, she and Atkins, as well as the rest of their band mates, were playing one of their normal shows. Every other weekend, Atkins gave Booker a ride home alternating with a band mate named Ernie Holcomb. This night was Holcomb's night to drive her home, but Booker told Holcomb not to bother because she had a ride set up with an old classmate who was visiting, Paul Martin. Atkins never knew of this change of plans, and until he received a call the next morning he assumed Booker had left with Holcombe, as usual.

Martin's 1946 Ford Coupe was found at 6:30 the next morning by the Weaver family, who were on their way through Texarkana to Prescott, Arkansas. The keys were found still in the car's ignition. Several miles away, in Spring Lake Park, their bodies would be found. Neither the car nor their bodies were anywhere near their destination that night.

Band and classmates claimed that the two were never close to being a couple, and that Booker felt obligated to go out with Martin because of their connection at school. However, no one knows what they were doing pulled over that night, or why they were in that area of town in the first place. No matter what the true story was that night, Booker and Martin would be the Phantom Killer's third and fourth victims.

Like the previous attack, both victims were shot and killed with a .32 Colt semi-automatic revolver. And like the female targets before her, Booker had been sexually assaulted before her murder. After news of the murder was released, hundreds of Texarkana residents flooded the park, hoping to catch a glimpse of the crime scene or help the investigation.

Martin's body was found almost a mile and a half from the abandoned car. He had been shot four times and the ground surrounding his body was covered in his blood.

Booker's body would not be found until five hours later, over three miles from where the car had been found. Booker was found by the Boyd family and Ted Schoeppey, who had joined the community search party to help find the two teenage victims. Booker had been shot twice, and was found with her hand in her coat pocket.

Both bodies showed signs of a struggle against their attacker, yet their fight was unsuccessful. There was no conclusive evidence as to why their bodies were so far from their car.

Booker's missing saxophone played in the running theory of robbery as a primary motive. The police had alerts al over the area, asking people to keep an eye out for a pawned or for sale saxophone matching the serial number of Booker's, and for several months it was considered one of the best leads the authorities had on finding the killer. Unfortunately for the police, on October 24th, six months after Booker's murder, P. V. Ward and J. F. McNief found the saxophone still in its leather case, just yards from where Booker's body had been found. Ward claimed to know what it was as soon as they stumbled upon it. By the time the case and instrument were turned over to the police, the case had already been labeled closed.

A Red Herring

Public panic over the Phantom Killer was at its all-time high when Virgil and Katie Starks were attacked in their modest farmhouse just ten miles out of town. However, questions would eventually emerge over whether this was truly the work of the Phantom Killer, or if someone else was responsible for the crime.

On the quiet night of May 3[rd,] Virgil, 36, was reading the Texarkana Gazette when two gunshots burst through the front window of their ranch-style home. These bullets hit Virgil in the head, killing him instantly. Katie was lying in bed, already dressed in her nightgown, when she heard the sound of breaking glass. She headed for the living room, where her husband had been seated, only to find him slumped in his armchair, dead. She cried in fear as she reached for the phone, but the attacker shot through her lower jaw, spraying teeth fragments across the Starks kitchen.

In a state of panic and extreme pain, Katie managed to get back up to her feet. She attempted to grab her husband's gun, but was disoriented from being shot. Despite her injuries, she escaped from the house and ran for her sister's down the street. Finding the house empty, she continued to her neighbors' until she found refuge in the Prater house, where the police were finally called. When A. V. Prater answered the door, Katie simply said, "Virgil's dead," before collapsing on the ground. In the time it took for the police to arrive the killer had fled, taking no valuables or anything else of note with him.

Initially, this attack was labeled as another of the Phantom Killer's. It followed the same time pattern as his previous attacks, used a gun as the primary weapon, and targeted a couple. One of the biggest pieces of evidence connecting this attack to the Phantom Killer was a set of unfamiliar tire tracks that matched those found at the other crime scenes. Because of these similarities, many citizens of Texarkana insist that this murder and attempted assault was the Phantom Killer's final blow to the small town's community.

In November 1948, the local authorities made a different conclusion. Another man was arrested and charged with the home invasion and attack on Virgil and Katie Starks. Law enforcement referenced several reasons as to this not being the work of the Phantom Killer, including the fact that the weapon used was a .22 rifle. This change in weapon, as well as the fact this was a home invasion earlier in the evening, pointed police to consider a different suspect entirely.

The town is still home to many skeptics who believe this attack was the Phantom Killer's doing. The crime scene at the Starks home was filled with physical DNA evidence, but at the time DNA testing was only beginning to emerge in the most developed areas of the nation. A little town like Texarkana was nowhere near equipped to handle a case like this, and the DNA evidence was discarded or improperly stored for later testing. While the official stance is that the Phantom Killer was not involved in this attack, the question still haunts many in the area.

A Town In Panic

As the attacks added up, tension in the town of Texarkana grew. After the first and second attack, police forces from both states increased patrols on the town's secluded back roads. A community that had once been friendly, where front doors were never locked and neighbors were always welcome, now grew eerily quiet after sundown.

Businesses saw a decline in customers, especially those catering to the night crowd. Residents were afraid to leave home, even during the daylight, for fear they may become the next target of the Phantom Killer. However, one industry in town became a hotspot for concerned citizens – the local hardware and ammo shops.

Residents bought up guns and ammo like crazy, hoping to be able to defend themselves from the attacks. Deadbolts and other home security devices became commonplace in all the towns households, and some homeowners were even seen setting up booby traps and other contraptions to catch the killer in his tracks.

Many of the town's local high school and college boys rounded up patrol groups. These men would go out at night with baseball bats and other makeshift weapons, hoping to catch the Phantom Killer on the prowl. None of them were ever successful.

Rumors continued to spread and impair the investigations. There was constant news about someone's son being arrested for the murders, or a suspect being charged, but these rumors rarely ever revealed themselves to be true. Police were forced to perform damage control on the stories spreading around town while also conducting their own investigation into the attacks.

Under the Spotlight

After the final attack, at the Starks farmhouse, authorities and media swarmed into Texarkana like never before. The quiet town was buzzing with news reporters from all across the nation, and reports of the murders were spreading to all areas of the country. Texarkana had never experienced the media's curious eye before.

The famous Texas Rangers stepped into the investigation, headed by the well-known Manuel "Lone Wolf" Gonzaullas. Gonzaullas was the first Ranger captain from Spanish descent, and was known for being a ruthless charmer in his day. He spent a great of his time providing interviews for national newspapers and radio broadcasts about the state of the investigation. He was even found one day taking pictures of the Starks crime scene with a young *Life* magazine reporter; neighbors had reported suspicious lights and sounds from the house when Gonzaullas and the woman were found.

While the local press, headed by the Texarkana Gazette, dubbed the suspected serial killer the "Phantom Killer" or "Phantom Slayer," national media clung to a different name: "The Moonlight Murderer." Because of this title, many believe that the murders were all committed under the full moon, when the nights were in fact at their darkest during the time of the crimes.

A Fruitless Investigation

The entire nation was on the lookout for a masked killer terrorizing young couples, with leads coming in from all areas of the South. In all, the authorities considered over four hundred separate suspects, but no one was ever charged with the attacks of that spring. While most of these suspects never received any public attention, the media caught wind of some of the more notable ones.

A middle-aged man from College Station, a Texas town several miles west of Texarkana, was at one point considered a prime suspect. He had previously been caught sneaking up on parked cars, typically with young couples inside, and brandishing a .22 rifle in order to threaten and rob them. While this man was never convicted of murder, many believed him to be the Phantom Killer based on the similar crime and weapon.

In Fayetteville, a young male graduate student of the University of Arkansas committed suicide. In the wake of his untimely death, a note was found containing a handwritten poem and confession to the murders in Texarkana. His military records showed he had showed "homosexual tendencies" during his time with the U.S. Navy, and at the time these tendencies were believed to be a mental disorder related to sexual crimes like rape or assault. Nothing of value ever came from this lead.

Several local residents accused an IRS agent of the crimes, seemingly because of his antisocial demeanor or because he had gotten on the town's bad side. Another man claimed to have committed the crimes during fits of amnesia. Neither of these claims resulted in an arrest.

In 1999 and 2000, several years after the last murder, an anonymous woman called surviving family members of the Phantom Killer's victims, claiming to be his daughter. She apologized for the actions of his crimes and begged for forgiveness from the families. There is speculation over whether these claims are valid, but many believe them to simply be a cry for attention. After all, the primary suspect of the Phantom Killer murders, Youell Swinney, never had a daughter.

Chasing a Criminal

During his time investigating the Moonlight Murders, Max Tackett, an Arkansas law officer, made a puzzling connection. Before each murder a car had been reported stolen and subsequently abandoned on the side of the rode. This information led police to believe that the Phantom Killer was using stolen vehicles to flee the crime scenes, and then dumping them before disappearing into the night.

The next car reported stolen triggered a police stakeout, with law enforcement hoping to find the killer connected to the vehicle. As police closed in on the stolen vehicle, Peggy Swinney was found to be driving. Police seized the car and took Peggy into custody, where she was questioned on how she came to possess the stolen vehicle.

Peggy revealed that Youell Swinney, a known car thief in Texarkana, had given the car to her, but that wasn't all she had to say. Peggy began telling police how Youell was the Phantom Killer, how he had assaulted and murdered all those couples, and how he had made her promise not to tell anyone. She included details of the crimes that had not been given to the public, information only known by police and the killer himself.

Before the police could move in on Youell Swinney, Peggy's story changed. She claimed that her previous confession was a lie, and that Youell was not the Phantom Killer after all. Eventually law enforcement discovered that Peggy and Youell had recently been married, making her unable to testify against her husband at all. While Youell remained an unofficial suspect, it seemed that the police were unable to touch him. But that changed in 1947, when Youell was arrested for auto theft.

At that time, Youell Swinney already had a long criminal record. He had been previously charged with counterfeiting, burglary, and assault, landing him in the Texas State Penitentiary for many years. After his release, he continued his work as a career criminal, but avoided capture for the time being.

During the investigation, police found evidence that Youell had owned a .32 Colt revolver, the murder weapon used to kill the second and third sets of victims, but that he had recently lost the gun in a failed card game. In hi home was also a shirt with the name "Stark" embroidered on the pocket, but it is unknown whether this shirt was actually connected to the Starks murder in the previous year.

With Youell in custody for auto theft, the police attempted to pin him as Texarkana's Phantom Killer. The man had a history of violence and sexual assault, and the record of stolen cars pointed toward his involvement in the murders. Youell never denied his innocence; he simply stayed quiet and refused to work with the police when questioned. A botched injection of "truth serum" during an interview in Little Rock, Arkansas, would eventually end the authorities' questioning of Youell regarding the Moonlight Murders. He was placed in prison for auto theft.

Youell remained in prison until 1973. Many of his cellmates recounted stories that Youell had told them, ones that included intimate details of the Phantom Killer's murder scenes and heavily suggested that Youell knew more than he let on. In 1994, Youell died a free man, never admitting to the Texarkana murders. To this day, most consider Swinney to be the Phantom Killer, even if he never served time for these crimes.

The Missing Woman

On June 1st, 1948, 21-year-old Virginia Carpenter departed Texarkana by train, on her way to her first semester of studying at the Texas State College for Women. She left Union Station at about 3PM, and headed for Denton, Texas and her new life as an educated woman. On the train ride, she met another student by the name of Marjorie Webster, who she shared a taxi with on the way to their dormitories.

Their taxi driver, Edgar Ray "Jack" Zachary, first dropped off Webster at the Fitzgerald dormitories, and then continued on to Brackenridge Hall, where Carpenter would be staying for the term. Zachary reported seeing Carpenter approach two young men in a yellow convertible outside the dorm, saying that she seemed to recognize them and was excited to see them. The next day, Zachary returned to the dorms to deliver some of Carpenter's luggage that she had forgotten at the station. He placed the trunk at the hall's front entrance and left, but no one ever claimed the luggage. That previous night would be the last time Virginia Carpenter was seen.

On June 4th, Carpenter's boyfriend, Kenny Branham, and her mother reported Virginia missing. After being brushed off by authorities, Mrs. Carpenter and other family members left for Denton late in the evening, hoping to help the police find Virginia.

Within several days, there were airplanes, motorboats, and on-foot search parties scanning the surrounding area for any sign of Virginia. Drivers of yellow convertibles were stopped and questioned, and Zachary was questioned by police and subjected to a polygraph test. Carpenter quickly became one of the most famous missing person cases in Texas, with her picture circulating across the country.

Before long, rumors started spreading back in Texarkana. Virginia Carpenter had personally known three of the Phantom Killer's victims, and some started to believe that she had a target on her back. Perhaps the killer had followed her from Texarkana to Denton, just another passenger on the crowded train. Or perhaps the killer was someone that Carpenter knew, like one of the men seen in the yellow convertible to night she went missing. Either way, many believe that this disappearance was connected to the attacks in 1946.

Countless sightings of Carpenter across Texas - riding in a car, buying groceries, or hitchhiking - continued to flow in, but no solid leads were ever discovered. By 1955, Carpenter was considered dead. She had been missing for seven years, and little hope remained of finding her. Despite this, tips continued to emerge on Carpenter's possible whereabouts.

In 1959, a wooden box was found buried with female remains inside that matched Carpenter's physical description. They were sent to Austin for examination, but the landowners soon confessed to digging them up from an old cemetery.

In 1998, a man called the police claiming to know where Carpenter's body was buried. He led police to the grounds of the Texas State College for Women, the school she was meant to attend, but the search came up empty.

Carpenter's disappearance causes some to doubt Youell Swinney's guilt. If her disappearance was a result of the Phantom Killer, the same man who brutally attacked at least three different couples, then this man could not be Swinney. At the time Carpenter went missing, Swinney was being held in prison for auto theft. Maybe Peggy Swinney had a hand in the disappearance of Carpenter, or her abduction was committed by someone other than the Phantom Killer, but it could not have been Swinney.

Phantoms Around the World

Some believe that the Phantom Killer simply moved his crimes to a new location, but it is likely he just inspired other killers to follow his pattern of attack. As the United States reached the height of violent crime and serial killers, attacks cropped up across the country and even abroad. The Phantom Kiiler's *modus operandi* (or M.O.) would become commonplace among serial killers in the coming decades, including the Zodiac Killer, Il Mostro, and the Son of Sam.

In 1946, a young couple was shot in Fort Lauderdale, Florida. Elaine Eldridge and Lawrence Hogan were parked outside Dania Beach when someone approached the vehicle and shot both victims with a .32 semi-automatic handgun. While the weapon used was not a Colt, it remained very similar to the one used in Texarkana. No fingerprints or footprints were found at the scene. With several similarities to the Texarkana attacks, many believed that the killer had relocated across the country. Texas, Arkansas, and Florida police worked together on the investigation, but no major connections were ever revealed to the public.

Located in San Francisco, the Zodiac Killer operated very similarly to the Phantom Killer during the late 1960s. He stalked young people in their vehicles and shot them with a revolver, and his identity remains unknown. However, unlike the Phantom Killer who personally avoided the media's attention, the Zodiac Killer was hungry for exposure. His main source of fame comes from sending cryptic notes to the Bay Area press, including four ciphers. Only one of these ciphers was ever solved, but it led the police no closer to identifying a suspect. These notes were examined top to bottom, in hopes of finding the true identity of the Zodiac Killer, but no leads were ever found.

Across the Atlantic Ocean, from 1968 to 1985, Florence, Italy was shook by sixteen murders. Dubbed Il Mostro or The Monster of Florence, the killer shot young couples parked alone in their cars with a .22 rifle. While four different suspects were arrested and charged with these murders throughout the years, the investigation has attracted scrutiny and many believe these men were actually innocent.

While the Son of Sam's identity is known today, his killings reflected those of the Phantom Killer and others. Operating in New York City in the mid 1970s, David Berkowitz killed six victims with a .44 Bulldog revolver. His attacks triggered the biggest manhunt in New York City, and for years women kept their hair short and avoided disco clubs for fear of being Berkowitz's next target. Like the Zodiac Killer, Berkowitz loved taunting the police and media with cryptic letters, where he promised to continue killing until he was caught. After his capture in 1977, Berkowitz enjoyed a bit of morbid celebrity for his crimes, which many reported he seemed to enjoy greatly. He remains in prison today, serving six life sentences.

While it is unlikely that the Phantom Killer actually relocated to be the Zodiac Killer or Il Mostro, some true crime experts believe it is possible. While the Phantom Killer was one of the first of his kind, looking back his killings were not exceptionally unique by today's standards.

It is easy to see how the Phantom Killer and his Moonlight Murders have shaped our ideas of killers today. Urban legends of a mad man stalking young couples in love, scratching on car doors and leaving bloody hooks behind, persist around campfires and in dark corners of the Internet. *The Town That Dreaded Sundown* might live among the likes of Freddy Krueger and Michael Myers, but it is a fictionalized retelling of the very real horrors that haunted Texarkana that year.

Bonus story

They called him the 'Railroad Killer.'

Angel Resendiz earned the nickname because of his penchant for committing his crimes near railroads, using the rail cars as his own personal get-away system.

Committing murder after murder, he was able to elude both American and Mexican authorities for over a decade.

EARLY LIFE

A birth certificate found by the FBI listed his date of birth as August 1st, 1960. He was born To Virginia de Maturino in the town of Izucar de Matomoros in the state of Puebla, Mexico. His mother has stated adamantly that the correct spelling of his surname is Recendis not Resendiz although the killer would have over fifty different aliases throughout his lifetime.

Angel had spent his childhood years with relatives and not with his immediate family. According to his mother, he was sexually abused by an uncle and other pedophiles in the town of Puebla. He would spend his youth roaming the streets, robbing, stealing and sniffing glue. Relatives would later testify that Resendiz was routinely beaten as a child, one time being "jumped" by several other youths who beat him so bad that he bled through his ears. Resendiz would leave home for months at a time then suddenly return mumbling about a coming religious apocalypse.

Legal trouble came early for Resendiz as he was caught trying to sneak into the Texas border at the age of sixteen. This would become the first of numerous run-ins with border patrol agents until he finally made it into the United States, making his way to St. Louis and finding work with a manufacturing company under an assumed name. He even registered to vote with his false identification.

In September of 1979, at the age of nineteen, Resendiz was arrested for assault and car theft in Miami. He was tried and sentenced to twenty-years in prison but was released after only six years and sent back to Mexico.

But he wouldn't stay there for long.

Through numerous attempts of trial and error, Resendiz had learned not only to game the system but to enter and exit the United States with minimal detection.

He learn to use the rail-cars...

AN "INVISIBLE" MAN

Resendiz became so skilled at crossing the border without detection that he began charging for his services. He began to make a living as a human smuggler, transporting Mexicans across the border for a fee.

Resendiz soon developed a reputation for his smuggling skills, often being seen as a 'go to' person in his Ciudad Juarez neighborhood called 'Patria.'

He would make weekly crossings over the border, being arrested only intermittently. He would then be deported back into his native land only to ping-pong back and forth.

Finally, Resendiz would serve prison terms for his crimes. He would be arrested in Texas for false identity and citizenship, getting a year and half worth of jail.

Upon release in 1987, he journeyed to New Orleans and was arrested for carrying a concealed weapon. He received another year and half worth of prison time until parole.

He then went back to his old haunts in St. Louis where he tried to defraud Social Security and receive illegal payments. He got caught and served a three year sentence.

Resendiz then decided small-time burglaries were his deal. He once again illegally crossed the border, journeyed to New Mexico and was caught burglarizing a home. He was imprisoned for eighteen months and upon release he broke into a Santa Fe rail yard, being captured yet again.

"They should have called Resendiz the boomerang man," forensic psychologist Frank Lizzo said. "He knew how to play the game and seemingly had no fear of the system. The system never punished him severely enough for him to stop his crimes, let alone stop crossing the border."

After his last recorded deportation, the killings began.

THE KILLING FIELDS

"He probably started killing somewhere in his late 20s," Douglas said. "He may have killed people like himself initially – males, transients...(he) became angry at the population at large. What America represents here is this wealthy country where he keeps getting kicked out...(he) just can't make ends meet. Coupled with these feelings, these inadequacies, fueled by the fact that he's known to take alcohol, take drugs, lowers his inhibitions now to go out and kill."

Angel's list of victims began in 1986. Continuing to bounce in and out of the United States, he shot a homeless woman and left her for dead in an abandoned farm house. He had met the acquaintance of the woman at a homeless shelter and they became friends. They would later take a trip on a motorcycle together when he felt that the woman disrespected him.

Resendiz would then take out his gun and blow her head off.

The woman allegedly had a boyfriend whom Resendiz shot and killed as well. He said that he dumped his body in a creek between San Antonio and Uvalde. This killing has never been verified aside from what Resendiz revealed to the police during his interrogation sessions.

Five years later, Resendiz would kill Michael White because he was a "homosexual." Resendiz would bludgeon White to death with a brick and leave him in front of an abandoned home.

These were seemingly warm-ups for the more brutal crimes to come which would also include rape.

"Sex seemed almost secondary," FBI profiler John Douglas said when apprised of Resendiz's crimes. "(He is) just a bungling crook ...very disorganized."

Douglas would later concede, however, that it was this disorganization that worked in his favor. Like a true drifter, Resendiz' whereabouts became as elusive as a rational thought in his head.

"When he hitches a ride on the freight train, he doesn't necessarily know where the train is going," Douglas said. "But when he gets off, having background as a burglar, he's able to scope out the area, do a little surveillance, make sure he breaks into the right house where there won't be anyone to give him a run for his money. He can enter a home complete with cutting glass and reaching in and undoing the locks."

"He'll look through the windows and see who's occupying it. The guy's only 5 foot-7, very small. In fact...the early weapons were primarily blunt-force trauma weapons, weapons of opportunity found at the scenes. He has to case them out, make sure he can put himself in a win-win situation."

Resendiz would also leave his weapon of choice up to chance. Whatever the home would have, a statue a mantle piece, a butcher knife, that would become the instrument of murder.

FLORIDA KILLINGS

On March 23rd, 1997, Jesse Howell would be found bludgeoned to death beside the railroad tracks in Ocala, Florida. He was nineteen years old.

"When we got there," Sheriff Patty Lumpkin said. "We see what appears to be a young male, in his late teens or early twenties. Blood around the head area. You could tell by looking at him that he was dead. The first thing I do is make sure that we've got our forensics people on the way, on the medical examiners on the way, and all the investigators that we have called out or either there or en route."

"When those types of things happen it might have been someone who had fallen off a train," Lt. Jeff Owens said. "Or someone who could have been struck by a train."

The authorities quickly ruled out an accident, however, as they examined the body.

"It didn't appear to be an accident," Lumpkin said. "Because if he had been hit by the train the trauma would have been much more extreme. I've seen some deaths from trains and the initial impact from the train would have done more harm to the body."

The forensic team did determine that Howell's body looked as if he were the victim of blunt force trauma.

"We did see a baseball type of cap," forensic scientist Michael Dunn said. "It appeared to have blood on the inside surface of he bill. In addition, there was a pair of wire rimmed eye glasses and one of the eye pieces was missing, one of the lenses was out. This didn't look good either. As we moved closer, we saw that the victim had been dragged to that spot using just the blue jean material around the cuff (of his pants)."

Near the body, they found a brass and rubber coupling. This device was used to link one train car to another. It could also be used as a clubbing weapon.

"It had what appeared to be blood on it (the coupling)," Dunn recalled.

Howell still had jewelry on his person. He wore a gold cross necklace, a watch and a small amount of cash in his pocket. The police ruled out robbery as a motive.

The police did not identify Howell's body right off the bat. They did find a money wire receipt where some money had been wired from Illinois to Florida. The name on the receipt was of a woman named "Wendy."

Police tracked the money transfer to its point of origin which was all the way in Woodstock, Illinois.

Coincidentally, the authorities there were investigating the disappearance of Wendy Von Huben.

Wendy was missing alongside her boyfriend, the nineteen year old Jesse Howell.

"They advised me that they were investigating a John Doe," Woodstock Detective Kurt Rosenquest recalled. "Unidentified male."

Rosenquest then followed up with the investigating team in Florida, sending them the fingerprints and pictures of Jesse Howell.

The Ocala police would then positively identify Howell.

Jesse had met Wendy only months earlier. They had secretly planned to marry and went on a road trip with another couple.

The other couple, however, grew tired of Jesse and Wendy's constant bickering. They demanded to be let out of the car and left. Jesse and Wendy continued into Ocala, Florida where they ran out of money.

Wendy would call her parents in Illinois who would then transfer her $200 via Western Union. The couple would collect the $200 but would not return home.

"We checked Greyhounds," Rosenquest said. "Nobody matching their description ordered buses or train tickets back to the Woodstock area."

Tears were shed as Rosenquest informed Howell's parents that their teen son had been murdered. The investigative team then turned their attention to the disappearance of Wendy.

They held out hope because there were issues between her and Jesse, thinking that perhaps she simply ran off to be by herself.

Police scoured the surrounding areas and used helicopters in all directions around the railroad tracks.

They would find nothing. There was no DNA left behind on Jesse Howell's body either.

Papers and fliers with Wendy Von Huben's information was distributed all throughout Florida up through Illinois.

Authorities also began interviewing the transient population that lived along the railroad tracks.

Two and a half months later, however, Wendy's parents would receive a phone call.

"The phone rang," Rosenquest recalled. "Wendy's father answered the phone. The girl was crying. She said 'I'm sorry. I love you.'"

She would tell the father she was two hours away from Woodstock at a gas station. The father asked for the phone number on the pay phone she was calling from and she said that there wasn't any before hanging up.

The police were not certain that the phone call came from Wendy so they immediately headed out to the gas station where they believe the call took place.

Police tracked down the surveillance video of the gas station. On the video, a woman that physically resembled Wendy entered the gas station.

The phone records, however, revealed that the call did not come from the gas station where the surveillance video revealed a woman who allegedly was Wendy. It came from another gas station where there were fliers posted of Wendy.

Someone had played a cruel hoax as Wendy's parents had added their home number to the fliers

ONE-LEGGED BOB AND A CHANCE DISCOVERY

A year went by without any sign of Wendy.

There was some ray of hope, however, as the railroad authorities called the Ocala police and informed them that the received information from a member of one of the homeless camps. They had a man in custody named "One Legged Bob" who was traveling with a girl and may be responsible for the murder of her previous boyfriend.

"'One Legged Bob' was your typical homeless person," Owens said. "Kinda scruffy. Hadn't shaved in a few days. He had a prosthetic leg that helped him get around. For someone who you might consider crippled, he was far from crippled."

Owens would spend the next eight hours interviewing the only lead he had, a one legged homeless man.

After the grueling interrogation, Owens realized that he had the wrong suspect.

By sheer chance, however, Patty Lumpkin heard about someone they dubbed the "Railroad Killer" during a class she was taking at the FBI.

"They called him the Railway Killer," Lumpkin recalled. "The Angel of Death. He was killing people. Leaving them near the railroad or he was killing them at homes or locations that were close to the railroad.

The FBI knew the Railway Killer as Angel Resendiz.

"We knew that Angel Resendiz was a person that rode the rails across the country," FBI Agent Mark Young said. "We were worried where he'd wind up next. So we decided to make him a top ten fugitive. Maybe the millions of eyes of the public would tell us something."

The strategy worked.

"He was one of the most vile, evil persons that I had ever dealt with," Young said. "It was like every time you turn around there's another murder."

Owens and Lumpkin hoped to talk to Resendiz to query him about Jesse Howell's murder and Wendy Von Huben's disappearance.

"The attorneys representing him at the time in Texas stopped us," Owens said. "They wanted to protect their client from talking. Any defense attorney who represents a criminal will generally tell the person to stop talking to law enforcement."

Resendiz was placed on death row and Texas had a fast execution rate. The two detectives worried that they would lose their chance to interview Resendiz and connect him to the crimes in Ocala.

Owens and Lumpkin decided to mail Resendiz a letter, respectfully asking him if they could interview him. The letter was written in a formal manner and even addressed him as "Senor."

To their surprise, Resendiz responded back and granted them an interview regarding his involvement in Jesse's killing and Wendy's disappearance.

During their meeting, Resendiz was quick to admit that he had killed Jesse. The detectives deliberately withheld information about the killing, holding back details that only the killer would know. But when Resendiz described using a brake coupling from one of the trains, they knew they had their killer.

But they needed to find out what happened to Wendy.

In a follow-up letter, they promised him immunity from prosecution if he agreed to talk. It was a moot point by then as he was already on death row but the detectives still needed permission from Wendy's family to go through with the interview.

In order to receive some sense of closure, the family agreed to the immunity.

"When we get to the prison," Lumpkin said. "We see him coming down the hallway. He (Resendiz) has a waist belt on. It's an electric shock belt and he's chained to the belt. He's just a mild-mannered person but remember that a psychopath or a sociopath doesn't have any feeling. I mean he had dead eyes. He had no feeling in that body. He didn't care about anything."

Resendiz would reveal that he was heading south for work when the train stopped and he spotted Jesse getting off the train for a smoke.

"Resendiz told us that he killed Jesse with a piece of the train coupling," Lumpkin said. "And Wendy was asleep on the train when this took place. And then when they went down the road further somehow he talked Wendy into getting off the train."

Resendiz then raped and strangled Wendy to death.

Resendiz drew a map of where had left Wendy's body. He described burying her in a shallow grave near a canopy of trees. Resendiz would remember that she had a book in a back pack and an army style jacket that he used to cover her fresh grave.

Police would return to the site and were able to locate where he buried Wendy's body. Almost three years after the murder, everything the killer described was still there. The book. The jacket.

And Wendy's body.

"When Wendy ran away she had a small engagement ring," Owen said. "And she had a Winnie the Pooh wristwatch."

The detective would bring those items back to Wendy's parents.

KENTUCKY RAILROAD MURDER

In August of 1997, Resendiz would make his way from Ocala, Florida to Lexington, Kentucky. It was there he would stalk two young college students.

Holly Dunn was a 20-year old junior at the University of Kentucky and it was there she met Christopher Maier.

"Chris Maier was my very good friend," Dunn recalled. "He was just the nicest, kindest man. We decided that we wanted to be more than friends then we started dating. We dated for about three months."

"Chris and I were attending a party. We decided that the party wasn't very fun so we went to go talk a walk by the railroad tracks. We sat down and talked for awhile and when we got up to leave a man came out from behind an electrical box. He had a weapon that he used on Chris. It was some sort of ice pick or screw driver. Something sharp. I guess our immediate thought was he's going to rob us. That's when we realize he wants money we start thinking 'okay, well, you could have our credit card, you can have our ATM card, you can have our car.' Then he started tying up Chris' hands behind his back. And then he came over to me and he took off my belt and that's when I started thinking he doesn't want to rob us."

After tying up Holly, Resendiz then pulled Chris by the shirt across the railroad tracks and into a ditch.

Holly would follow on her knees, pleading for him to stop whatever he was about to do.

"Lie down," Resendiz said, his voice soft but menacing.

"Everything is going to be okay," Christopher said to Holly as Resendiz dragged him into the ditch.

"Shut up!" Resendiz commanded as he gagged Christopher with a sock.

Resendiz then walked off into the darkness. The frightened couple did not know what the psychopath had planned.

"Then he comes with this rock," Holly recalled. "There was no warning, he drops this rock on Chris' head. I'm just thinking 'what just happened?' I don't even know what just happened."

"You don't have to worry about him anymore," Resendiz said to Holly as he got on top of her.

"I went into survival mode, I'm thinking, I mean he's gonna kill me. I may as well fight. I'm gonna fight. He unties my feet and climbs on top of me. I start to kick and scream and hit him but he held that knife or ice pick (to my throat) and said 'look how easily I could kill you.' I stopped everything and then he raped me."

"I memorized his face," Dunn said. "I stared at him and memorized, he had a tattoo on his arm, I was thinking if you have any scars I'm gonna remember your scars, I'm gonna remember your face, I'm not gonna forget it because if I live through this I will get you."

Resendiz completed the sexual assault of Dunn before smashing her head with a rock.

"He hit me five or six times in my face," Dunn recalled. "I think I put my hand up and then I turned over and then he hit me five or six times in the back of my head. He hit me hard. He was trying to kill me. I think I laid there and he thought I was dead."

Resendiz did think she was did as he threw the rock down and ran away from the crime scene.

Holly would suffer severe facial trauma but miraculously survived the attack.

"I had a broken jaw," Dunn said. "Broken eye socket and cuts on the back of my head that they had to staple shut and then I had cuts on my face."

She woke up in a Kentucky hospital, surrounded by family members.

"Everyone was told not to talk about Chris to me. I just said 'Chris is dead, isn't he?' And my Dad actually is the one I said that to and he was like 'yes, he died.'"

TEXAS TERROR

Resendiz would travel to Texas via train and in October of 1988 he flopped down in Hughes Springs. He would enter the home of 87-year old Leafie Mason, attacking the woman with an iron and killing her.

Two months later, Resendiz would sneak into the home of Dr. Claudia Benton, a thirty-nine year old medical researcher who lived in a suburb of Houston near the railroad tracks.

Again, it was a case of a home being to close to the train tracks. The train would provide the perfect cover for the sneaky Resendiz as he realized that the sound of the rail-car racing by would allow him to break in homes without being heard.

He applied the same technique with Benton, breaking into her home, raping then killing her.

Police would find the doctor face down on the floor. Her bedroom soaked in blood, ransacked for any valuables.

He head had been covered in a plastic bag while her body had been covered in a blanket.

"It appears that she (Claudia Benton) was sleeping," recalled Ken Macha, former police sergeant. "He was able to get in and picked up a bronze statuette from the mantle in the living room. He was relentless in beating her. The skull fractures themselves would have been enough to kill her. She was then stabbed in the back with a very large butcher knife."

"Resendiz was brutal, sadistic," said former West University police chief Gary Brye.

Fingerprints and DNA evidence would link Resendiz to the crime.

The problem was they could catch the man that Texas Ranger Drew Carter referred to as "a walking, breathing form of evil."

EVADING POLICE

Seven months later, Resendiz would continue to avoid capture. He remained in Texas, riding the rail cars until coming into the town of Weimar. He would break into the home of Pastor Norman "Skip" Sirnic and his wife Karen. Resendiz smashed a jack hammer into both of their heads, killing them instantly. He would then rape the body of Karen postmortem.

"He would watch these places," prosecuting attorney Devin Anderson said. "He would watch them, wait for them to go to sleep, get in their house and he would strike them before they would even wake up. I thought we have got to catch this guy."

The DNA found at the scene of the Sirnic murders would match those left on Benton. The FBI then realized they had a highly mobile serial killer on the loose...someone who could kill in one town then appear in another town miles away and kill again.

Resendiz was also smart. He would constantly alter his appearance. He'd shave his head. Then his mustache. He'd be clean shaven one week. Unkempt the next. He would wear glasses one week. No glasses the next.

Authorities could not get an accurate description of him other than the fact that he was small.

Resendiz was also able to take advantage of the lack of a coordinated computer system that gave law enforcement the ability to cross-check fugitives. After the Sirnic murders, Border Patrol had encountered Resendiz near the El Paso border but did not find him on the wanted list.

They then deported him back to Mexico.

Within 48 hours, Resendiz was back across the border to resume his killing spree.

"Our computers told us that he was nothing of lookout material," said C.G. Almengor, a supervisor at the border."We really wish he had been in the system so we could have caught him."

Resendiz would be deported no less than seventeen times over the course of his rampage. At no point did authorities make the connection because of his changing appearance, use of different aliases and the lack of a connected system to document illegals trying to come across the border.

A PREFERENCE FOR TEXAS

Noemi Dominguez was a graduate of Rice University who had just recently quit her job as an elementary school teacher to pursue a master's degree.

She was described as "the sweetest, nicest teacher – a darling who went the extra mile."

Fueled by hate, Resendiz would break into Noemi's home and rape her before killing her with a pick ax. He then stole her car and drove to Schulenberg, Texas where he would kill Josephine Konvicka with the same pick ax.

He would leave the weapon embedded in Konvicka's head as well as leave his fingerprints all over the home. He was more than just sloppy, he was getting cocky. He left a newspaper article that described his crimes as well as a toy train...a reference to his nickname as the "Railroad Killer."

Resendiz was also meticulous in approaching his victims.

"He undid the light in her (Noemi's) car," Anderson said. "So when he opened the door it wouldn't come on. That's who were were dealing with. Someone who really knew how to sneak around. Who really knew how to avoid detection."

"He kept killing people. He would not stop. In his mode of transportation, using the railroads was brilliant because they couldn't be monitored. I mean there's thousands of trains and millions of miles of tracks all over the United States."

"I felt hopeless at the time. Because if you're willing to sleep in a train or you're willing to sleep in a field, you can stay lost for a long, long time and I didn't think we were ever going to catch him."

Later that month, Resendiz had journeyed to Illinois, reaching the town of Gorham. He would break into the home of 80-year old George Morber and his daughter Carolyn Frederick. Resendiz would tie Morber to a chair and shoot him in the back of the head with a shotgun. He then raped Carolyn and smashed the shotgun across her head with such force that the weapon broke in half.

Both Morber and Frederick would die from their injuries.

The FBI placed him on their Top Ten list.

They then recruited his common-law wife, Julietta Reyes, and brought her into Houston for questioning from her hometown of Rodeo, Mexico.

Reyes complied with police requests, turning over over ninety-three pieces of jewelry that her husband had mailed to her from the U.S.

Relatives of Noemi Dominguez claimed thirteen pieces. George Benton was able to identify some pieces of jewelry as belonging to his wife as well.

Police would then locate Resendiz's half-sister, Manuela Karkiewicz, who lived in New Mexico. Initially, she refused to cooperate. She worried that the FBI or the police would kill her brother. But Carter convinced her to talk Resendiz into giving himself up.

The FBI knew that Resendiz had made his way back to Mexico after the murders in Illinois and was hiding in his hometown neighborhood of Patria.

Carter was able to get a rapport with Manuela. He convinced her that Resendiz would receive "personal safety while in jail, regular visiting rights for his family and a psychological evaluation."

"I came away with the impression that they (Resendiz' family) definitely had an understanding of right and wrong ... and knew now that what Maturino Resendiz was accused of doing was heinous and wrong ... ," Carter said. "Manuela, especially, came across as a woman of strong faith. There was a very deep emotional strain and burden placed on her in this investigation. She had to make some very difficult choices that impacted her and her family. And, in the end, her actions alone speak to her character."

Carter spent weeks talking to Manuela who in turn "worked a miracle."

They got the serial killer to surrender.

On July 12th, Manuela would receive a fax from the district attorney's office in Harris County which formalized everything that Texas Ranger Carter had promised.

The word passed from Manuela to another relative who acted as a go-between with Resendiz. The relative than came back later that evening and said that Resendiz would surrender in the morning at 9 a.m.

Texas Ranger Drew Carter would accompany Manuela and a spiritual adviser to meet with Resendiz on a bridge that connected El Paso, Texas to Ciudad Juarez.

"When I saw that face there was a little bit of excitement there because I finally said, 'This is going to happen,'" Carter recalled as he remembered Resendiz appearing on the bridge with his dirty jeans, muddy boots and blank facial expression. "He stuck out his hand, I stuck out my hand, and we shook hands."

Resendiz would then surrender to the Texas Ranger.

DEATH PENALTY

Resendiz' attorneys knew that their only hope would be an insanity defense. The Mexican government also got involved, lobbying authorities to spare Resendiz the death penalty

"Insanity was the logical defense because no one wants to believe that there is someone out there who would do things like that," Anderson said. "That was the thing that worried me the most about the case was that jurors would just throw up their hands and say nobody in their right mind could do what he does."

"The thing about what a life sentence with Resendiz would have been, he would have enjoyed it. I mean he would have had pen pals. He would have given interviews if they let him, I mean he would have loved it. And I knew that. And he didn't deserve to live after what he did just didn't. He caused so much pain, so much heartache and so much terror, that's what the whole focus of the trial had to be."

George Benton, the husband of Claudia, would vehemently criticize the Mexican government who support his appeals and domestic opposition to the death penalty.

"(He)looked like a man and walked like a man. But what lived within that skin was not a human being."

"He was small," Anderson said when she first saw Resendiz in the courtroom. "Maybe five- foot five. His forearms though, were roped with muscles. He was scary. Even though he was small you could feel he was dangerous. He looked like a wild animal who'd been caught."

Resendiz looked "timid" in the courtroom and spoke of himself in religious riddles. He claimed he was Jewish and didn't seem effected when he was informed that the prosecution was aiming for the death penalty.

"I don't believe in death," Resendiz, said. "I know the body is going to go to waste. But me, as a person, I'm eternal. I'm going to be alive forever."

The defense said that Resendiz' crimes were caused by head injuries, drug abuse and a family history of mental illness. He has a delusional perception of the world as he believes that he can cause earthquakes, floods, and explosions and that God told him to kill his victims whom they believed to be evil.

He made a living stealing things from his victims and having his wife sell them in Mexico. "That was his job," Anderson said. "And for recreation it was killing the people who lived in the house."

"He was a very intelligent person who worked the system and knew exactly what kinds of things to say to get that defense to work."

The jury, however, would find Resendiz guilty after one hour and forty-five minutes of deliberation.

He was sentenced to die via lethal injection.

"He made it very clear during my conversation with him that he deserves to die," Owens said.

"I want to ask if it is in your heart to forgive me," Resendiz said in his final words. "You don't have to. I know I allowed the devil to rule my life. I just ask you to forgive me and ask the Lord to forgive me for allowing the devil to deceive me. I thank God for having patience with me. I don't deserve to cause you pain. You did not deserve this. I deserve what I am getting."

Resendiz then prayed in Hebrew and Spanish before drawing his final breath.

House of Horror : The True Story of Rosemary West

Mary Gilmore

Unfortunately, it's not unusual in this day and time to turn on the news and hear a warning about a new serial killer roaming our streets. It's horrifying and hard to comprehend what could possibly make a person commit such heinous crimes. What is wrong with this person that drives him or her to commit such an act? The truth is that people have searched for the answers to that question for a very long time. Unfortunately, it still remains a mystery for the most part.

Rosemary West is one of those baffling cases. We will look deeper into her life and learn how her inner demons progressed to becoming one of Britain's most notorious and sadistic serial killers, taking the lives of at least 10 young women and girls.

Most of the information obtained by the authorities came from her husband and partner in crime, victims who escaped or were permitted to leave, and a great deal from her own children. Rosemary has offered very limited insight into the story, even to this day.

Remarkably, she did not act alone in committing these grisly deeds. This story is immensely complex, which I will attempt to sort out and then tie it all together with the union of Rose Letts West and Fred West in their vicious killing spree. There will be accounts of child abuse, rape, sexual deviance, torture, and murder. Rosemary West's crimes were so horrendous; it may be difficult for some of you to read.

Rosemary West's Early Life

Rosemary's mother came into her room one morning to wake her for school. Rosemary probably knew by the familiar expression on her mother's face that this would be one of those mornings that fills her life with constant dread. As she gets dressed, she begins preparing herself for what she knows is probably about to occur.

As she walks into the kitchen, breakfast is the last thing on her mind. Instead, she braces herself for the punishment she is about to receive. Don't misunderstand, Rosemary hadn't done anything wrong, but her father didn't need a reason.

His kind of punishment wasn't a time-out or a swat on the behind as most children receive. His were the kind that affect a child for a lifetime. Rose has no idea whether she is about to be beaten or if she'll endure other horrors that her father is known to inflict.

That is a likely scenario in the life of Rosemary West. Her father was a paranoid schizophrenic. The mental illness along with other problems, made life for her, her mother, and her siblings a nightmare. The abuse was bad enough, but what made it even more terrifying was not knowing from one minute to the next when or why her father's rage would erupt.

As a result of her home life, Rose made bad grades and became overweight. To make her situation worse, she was teased and bullied at school, giving her no relief from the continuous damage to her self-esteem.

There's a possibility that Rosemary's destiny was sealed much earlier in her life. It's not surprising that Rosemary's mother suffered from severe depression. The illness was so debilitating that she received electroconvulsive therapy several times while Rosemary was still in the womb, one of which occurred just before Rosemary's birth. There were some that thought this therapy was the reason for Rosemary's frequent outbursts of anger as well as her inability to do well in school.

Most of us would be unable to imagine a childhood such as the one led by Rosemary West.

Why do They Kill?

There are no exact traits of a serial killer to help us understand what drives them to kill. Some of them come from a two parent loving home while others have divorced parents. Some had abusive parents and others had loving parents.

Some think it's due to a head or brain injury sometime in their life; however, most people that have had brain injuries do not become killers. The majority of serial killers are men who act alone. Rosemary is not only a woman, she also had a partner in her life of crimes. Female killers and couples represent only a small percentage of serial killings.

The Federal Bureau of Investigation did a symposium, which was comprised of 135 experts who have dealt with serial killers in various ways to determine commonalities of serial killings. They determined that there are no definitive common traits. However, the central nervous system is constantly developing in adolescence, which determines a person's social coping system. That is, they develop the way they interact with their peers such as in negotiation and compromise. If it does not develop adequately, it can result in violent behavior.

It would be safe to say that the events of Rosemary West's childhood could be a factor in the choices she made later in life.

Rosemary's Life Before the Murders

Rosemary Letts was the fifth child born to Bill and Daisy Letts in Devon, England on the 29th of November in 1953. She normally went by the shorter version of her name, Rose. As we've seen, Rose's childhood was unlike most other children's. In pictures of Rose at a younger age she had an ever present smile on her face. You wouldn't guess that she was going through hell within the walls of her home.

The Letts family lived in Northam, a charming seaside town in Devon. Neighbors thought of Bill Letts as a nice man; however, they must have thought it strange that they rarely saw his children. When they did, the children were mainly seen walking around in their garden. One neighbor stated that they really didn't seem to be playing at all. They were just walking around and rarely seen outside the walls of the garden.

What they didn't know was that the children weren't allowed outside the walls and were afraid to play because they were forbidden to get dirty.

Although Rose's father constantly punished the children including Rose, he was not as physically abusive with Rose as with his wife and the other children. It was thought that he didn't physically abuse her as much as the others because he thought there was something not quite right about her.

Some people thought that he didn't hurt Rose as much because he was using her for his sexual pleasures instead. Others speculated that Rose learned at a very young age that she could control her father's anger by using sex.

Rose's mother Daisy, eventually left her father. She moved out of their house taking Rose and the other children with her, freeing them from the abusive environment. Remarkably, after a brief time, Rose moved back in with her father who resumed sexually abusing her.

One day, as Rose waited for a bus, she was approached by a man. Rose described him as a dirty man who had disgusting green teeth. She and the man struck up a conversation and even though his appearance was repulsive by most people's standards, Rose became attracted to him. The man's name was Fred West.

West was raising his daughter and stepdaughter at that time so Rose began babysitting the two girls. In addition, Rose and Fred also became a couple.

Fred's Early Years

Fred West, the son of Walter and Daisy West, was born in Much Marcle, England in 1941. He was the second of their six children. Growing up, he was considered to be a nice boy. They appeared to be a normal family, however, Fred's upbringing was perhaps even worse than Rosemary's. According to Fred, the motto around his house by his father was, "Do whatever you want, just don't get caught."

Fred would later reveal to police that incest was a common occurrence in his household. He said his father regularly had sex with his own daughters. Fred also claimed that his father introduced him to bestiality. In addition, it was thought that his mother Daisy took his virginity when he was 12-years-old.

Not surprising, Fred did not do well in school and dropped out at the age of 15. Two years later, he was involved in a tragic motorcycle accident. He received a broken arm and leg and a fractured skull. The head injury put him in a coma for eight days. Afterward, his family claimed that thereafter, he frequently become enraged without warning. Amazingly, two years later, he received another head injury. In this instance, he fell from a fire escape causing unconsciousness for 24 hours.

Fred's history of child abuse and head injuries would certainly coincide with the conceivable characteristics of a serial killer.

At the age of 20, he was caught and arrested for molesting a 13-year-old girl who subsequently became pregnant. He was convicted, but for unknown reasons he was not sentenced to prison. The reason is possibly because the girl's parents and Fred's parents were friends. Even with his family's propensity for deviant sexual acts, they had recently decided to try their hand at getting religion, therefore, they disowned Fred after this latest incident.

Fred had problems keeping a normal job. He landed a construction job; however, he was caught stealing. In addition, he continued to get caught molesting more young girls. It's amazing how he could still be roaming the streets even back at that point.

Shortly after, when West was around 21, he ran into a former girlfriend named Catherine Costello. She was better known as Rena, which was the name she used while prostituting and the name stuck. In addition, Rena was an accomplished thief. Nevertheless, even with her reputation, she was described by neighbors and other acquaintances as a very nice person and an exceptionally good mother.

Even though she was already pregnant with another man's child at the time, things heated up between her and Fred again and they married about two months later. The baby girl was born in February

1963 and was named Charmaine. Rena had another child by Fred a year later and named her Anna Marie. You will hear the names of these two girls in a shocking context later in the story.

Unbelievably, someone gave Fred West a job driving an ice cream van. This wouldn't seem a proper job for Fred the child molester to say the least. For Fred, it was the perfect job with young girls running after him. It was an ideal way for him to find victims.

While working at this job, a four-year-old boy ran into the street in front of his van and the child was killed. After this incident, even though the death was accidental, Fred feared people in the area would seek retribution for the boy's death. He thought it would be in his best interest to move away.

At the time, a woman named Isa McNeil was caring for the West's children. Additionally, Rena had become friends with a young woman named Anne McFall. They all moved with Fred to *The Lakeside* caravan park in Bishop's Cleeve, Gloucestershire, which is where Fred would later live with Rose.

With Fred's sadistic habits still intact, there were soon problems in this odd household. Fred insistently pushed his warped sexual necessities onto all three women. It became too much for his wife, Rena, and the children's nanny, McNeil, so the two of them moved to Scotland. On the other hand, the other woman, Ann McFall, had warmed up to Fred and stayed behind. Besides, she had already become impregnated by him.

Fearful of Fred, Rena and Isa's planned was to keep their departure secret from him and sneak away. Unfortunately, McFall told Fred, which enraged him. He allowed them to leave, but not with the two children, so the two women fled to Scotland. Rena returned frequently to visit her children.

After that, McFall began to pressure Fred to divorce Rena and marry her. Apparently, this didn't set well with Fred. When she was eight months pregnant with Fred's child, she completely vanished. She was never reported missing, but her body was later discovered in a field minus her fingers and toes, which had been removed and were missing.

Fred was left to care for his daughter and stepdaughter.

The Evil Duo Unites

Around this time is when Fred met Rose at the bus stop. It was at the time when Fred was caring for his step-daughter and biological daughter, so Fred already had at least the one murder of Anne McFall under his belt when he met Rose. Rose then began taking care of the two children.

When they first got together Rose was only 16-years-old and Fred was 12 years older at 28. Her father absolutely disapproved of the relationship. He threatened West that if he didn't leave Rose alone he would call Social Services due to Rose's young age. That was ironic since her father had been having sex with her himself for a long time. Of course, that was most likely the reason he didn't want her to go.

Nevertheless, Rose moved in with Fred and they lived together as a family with Fred's two daughters. After only about two months, they married she moved in with him at *The Lakeside Caravan Park* in Bishop's Cleeve, Gloucestershire, where Fred had lived with Rena and Anne.

Of course Fred, a man of few scruples, soon introduced his young and damaged wife to a sadistic world of pornography and urged her into prostitution. Due to Rose's demoralizing childhood, it didn't take a lot of urging for her to become caught up in his world.

Not one to hold down a regular job, Fred's contribution to the income was mainly by thievery. He wasn't very accomplished at that either tand was frequently caught and arrested. It wasn't long before he was sent to prison for 10 months, leaving young Rose in charge of his two daughters.

To make matters worse, she had become pregnant and gave birth to her daughter, Heather, in 1970 while Fred was still in jail. Being young in addition to having mental problems, caring for three children was a tall order for Rose and she didn't handle the situation well, to say the least.

To add to the pressure, seven-year-old Charmaine, began to be unruly and Rose was unable to cope with it. Years later, according to the other child, Anna Marie, it was not unusual for both girls to receive severe beatings; however, no matter how bad the beating, Charmaine refused to cry. This infuriated Rose so it's no surprise that Charmaine didn't seem to be around any longer after that.

This is thought to be when Rose committed her first murder. Rose's tendency to lose her temper most likely caused her to loss control and kill Charmaine. Apparently, Rose hid the girl's body, because it's known that Fred disposed of the body after he returned from prison.

Fred would hold this over Rose in the future. On one of the occasions when Rose's father tried to convince her to leave Fred and come home, Fred made a remark that was something like, "Come on now Rose, you know what we have between us." For someone that didn't know Fred, it would sound like an expression of love. More than likely with Fred, it was his not so subtle way of saying, "You can't leave. I have too much on you." She later told her parents that Fred would do anything, including murder.

Fred's first undertaking after returning from jail was to dismembered and dispose of Charmaine's body. For whatever sick reason, as with Anne McFall, he removed her fingers and toes and then buried her. This became the normal process in Fred's body disposal. It was later speculated that Fred and Rose were possibly involved in Satan worship. It is thought by some that removing the fingers and toes of their sacrifices was typical for Satan worshipers.

The next time Rena Costello came to visit her daughter it naturally created a problem when she discovered her daughter's absence, thanks to Rose. As you can imagine, Rena was not happy about her missing daughter and demanded some answers. Therefore, Rose and Fred must have decided that Rena would have to go as well. So this visit to see her little girl resulted in Rena's demise as well. Minus her fingers and toes, she was buried in a field close to the Caravan Hotel where Rose and Fred still lived.

That meant a total of at least three people had already lost their lives courtesy of Fred and Rose West. One each for Rose and Fred and now Rena by both of them.

A brief time later, Rose gave birth to their second child, Mae. They bought a large two-story house in Gloucester; however, there was not much money coming in. Fred started putting up panels in the rooms to create multiple bedrooms called bedsits. They were tiny rooms, which didn't fit much more than a bed. They began renting out these rooms for extra income; however, the rooms served another purpose as well.

By this time, Rose's fulltime career had become *prostitute*. They also began working other women out of the house. One of the rooms labeled "Rose's Room" was dedicated to Rose for turning tricks. Outside the door was a red light, which was lit when the room was in business. The children knew they were not to disturb when the red light was on. The room also came complete with a peephole, which was Fred's method for watching his wife in action and for making videos.

Both Rose and Fred had come from a family where incest was normal. It was not unnatural to them when Rose's own father occasionally came to their house to have sex with her.

In around October of 1972, Rose and Fred hired Carol Owens as a new nanny for their children. She told her story years later stating that Fred and Rose attempted to bring her into their twisted lifestyle. Not wanting any part of it, she soon left their house.

A few weeks later, as she was walking home, Fred pulled up beside her and offered a ride. The next thing she knew he hit her on the head. When she awoke, her hands were tied and Fred was in the process of taping her mouth.

She was told that if she tried to resist, Fred would call in his friends and let them have their way with her and she would then be killed.

They said they would bury her under the paving stones outside their home along with hundreds of other girls. Terrified, she didn't attempt to resist.

Unbelievably, they allowed her to leave the next day and she proceeded to file charges on them. Fred somehow managed to convince the court that the sex was consensual. In addition, Owens decided that testifying against these two could be an unhealthy choice.

The couple was given a meager fine on a charge of indecent assault and then released. She would be the last victim that the Wests' would allow to leave alive.

Years later, she regretted not testifying. She felt that if she had, it could have saved the lives of numerous women and girls and she was most likely correct.

One day, Fred and Rose arrived home and their neighbor, Elizabeth Agius, was outside. She had become friendly with the couple, so Fred stopped for a chat. Just in conversation, she asked what they had been doing, so Fred proceeded to tell her exactly what they had been up to.

He said they were cruising around looking for young girls. He must have felt he needed to explain why his wife would go along with him on such an outing. He said they figured the girls would see Rose and wouldn't be scared to get in the car. She would later say that she thought he must be joking...he wasn't.

Meanwhile, Fred was busy redecorating the cellar. One of the prostitutes that worked in the house later told authorities that she saw black suits, masks, chains, and whips down there. Fred had created his own torture chamber.

Anna Marie, Fred's remaining child with Rena Costello, was the first to be brutalized in Fred's torture chamber. She was bound, gagged, and violently raped as Rose watched. She was only eight-years-old at the time and this treatment would continue for years.

Eventually, Anna Marie moved out of the house to live with her boyfriend, which quite possibly saved her life. Again, letting her go would prove to be a bad move for the Wests later in court. As one of the survivors, a considerable amount of the horror stories came from her.

After Anna Marie's departure, Fred's attentions naturally turned to his daughters Heather and Mae; however, Heather wanted no part of it and resisted. Understandably, she was unable to keep it to herself and told a friend about the horrors happening at home. This would seal her fate, but Fred later claimed to police that her death was accidental.

The life of Rose and Fred West continued filled with the unimaginable. They would go on to have a total of seven children who were born in a short time span. It is believed that three are by Fred, one is by her own father, and the remaining three are from her clients. It almost seemed that their reason for having children was so Fred and Rose would have someone to torture at the times when no one else was tied up in the cellar. You can certainly say with certainty that Fred and Rose West were definitely not loving parents.

The One's That Didn't Survive the Terror

Over the next few years, the abuse of the West's children continued as did the murders of others. At some point, Fred went to work at a slaughter house. It was thought that this is when his already violent habits became even more gruesome. It could have been a factor in his fascination for dismembering his victims.

It is believed the next victim was Lynda Gough who was a personal acquaintance of the West's. She enjoyed participating in some of their sexual activities by sharing sex partners with Rose. However, for unknown reasons she later vanished. Gough's mother came to the West's house looking her daughter and was told that she moved in order to pursue a job. While she was speaking to the woman, Rose was wearing some of Linda Gough's clothing.

Carol Ann Cooper, only 15-years-old, is thought to be the next victim. She disappeared while walking home from the movies.

Evidence showed she died by strangulation, was dismembered, and buried in the garden.

Lucy Partington was in town visiting her family and a friend over the Christmas holidays. She went to the bus station to take a bus back home and most likely Fred, being one to hang out at bus stations asked her if she wanted a ride. As Fred and Rose planned, it is thought that the only reason she let them even approached her was due to the presence of Rose.

It is thought that they kept Partington in captivity for about a week after she vanished because poor Fred showed up at the hospital about a week later with a large laceration needing stitches. Authorities think he received the cut while cutting up Partington.

Shirley Hubbard went missing when she was returning home from Droitwich. There was definitive evidence of her torture. Her head was completely wrapped with tape with only a short rubber tube in her mouth to breath.

Juanita Marian Mott was a former tenant of the Wests'. Her torture was obvious. She was gagged with a binding made of socks, tights, and a bra, which were all stuffed inside each other. She was also tied up with clothes line rope looped around her thighs, arms, wrists, and ankles. This was done with the rope going back and forth around her horizontally and vertically until she was completely immobilized. She also had a rope with a noose, which most likely suspended her from the rafters in the cellar.

Shirley Anne Robinson was one of the prostitutes that worked out of their house who had sexual relations with both Fred and Rose. She became pregnant by Fred, at the same time Rose was pregnant by one of her clients.

Shirley began to get the idea she would like to replace Rose, which is not advisable in this family. Rose demanded that she had to go. She and her unborn child were dismembered and buried in the back garden. The cellar was full of bodies by this time and the back garden became the new burial grounds.

Therese Siegenthaler was a hitchhiker in route from London to Ireland. Some of the evidence showed that like Partington, she was kept alive for close to a week during which time she was likely tortured and raped.

Allison Chambers was the last known non-related victim. She was killed in 1979.

Their oldest daughter, Heather Ann West, was the last known victim. Fred claims he killed her by accident. His story of the "accident" went something like this. He told police that Heather was being extremely insolent so he had to slap her. She then started laughing at him so he was forced to grab her by the throat to stop her from laughing. He said that unfortunately, he must have grabbed her too tightly because she began to turn blue and stopped breathing. He tried to revive her by putting her in the tub and running cold water on her, but it didn't work.

He then removed her clothes and attempted to put her in a garbage bin, but she didn't fit. Back into the tub she went so he could make her smaller, but he first strangled her with a cord to make sure she was dead. He told police he didn't want to start cutting her up and then have her come alive on him.

He also closed her eyes before he started cutting. He said he couldn't dismember her while she was looking at him. He must have been hearing a strange sound because he told police he found the source of a noise when he cut off her head. He said it was a horrible and unpleasant sound like scrunching. He also said that after cutting her up, she fit quite nicely into the garbage bin.

She was later put in a hole that the West's son, Stephen, had dug with the intention of it becoming a fishpond. Fred put Heather in the hole and built a patio over it. Stephen had unknowingly dug the grave for his own sister's burial.

Police also believed that they killed 15-year-old Mary Bastholm in 1968, though they never found her body. The Wests' son Stephen, later told authorities that he believes Bastholm was one of his father's earlier murders because his father boasted about it.

The Evidence Begins to Surface

Oddly, they violently murdered many of their victims, but then set others free after they had finished using and abusing them. Naturally, some of them went to the police.

The released victims were some extremely lucky women to say the least. Their reports finally got the attention of a Detective Constable named Hazel Savage. Savage was also familiar with Fred West and his arrests for thievery and child molestation through the years since the time he was married to Rena Costello.

Fred videoed an incident in which he raped Anna Marie while Rose held her arms. Anna Marie told friends about her home life who in turn told their parents. This and other information got back to Savage.

This enabled the Detective to obtain a warrant to search the West's property. It was the beginning of the needed evidence to finally remove these damaged and dangerous monsters from the unsuspecting public.

Fred was arrested and charged with rape and sodomy of a minor and Rose for assisting in the rape of a minor. Amazingly, Fred and Rose West were still not suspected of murder. At this time, the younger children were removed from the home.

Due to the evidence found in the home, Detective Savage had the suspicion that there was more going on here and she began digging deeper into this strange family. She had a feeling that there was something suspicious concerning the whereabouts of their daughter Heather and she was determined to find out.

For instance, it was noticed in the videos of the West's and their children that was seized from their home that Heather was never present. Also, in interviews with some of the children, they said something that should not come from the mouths of children.

Apparently, there was a common joke around the West house. Fred told the children that he would buried them under the patio with their sister Heather if they didn't behave.

Unbelievably, the case fell apart when two of the main witnesses decided not to testify. Detective Savage continued questioning the children repeatedly to no avail. Fred and Rose had programmed them and put enough fear in them by then that they would no longer say anything to help the case.

However, the evidence together with case workers reporting the family joke about their sister Heather kept Detective Savage searching. It also appeared that another child, Charmaine, was missing as well. Eventually, Savage put together enough evidence to obtain a warrant to dig on the Wests' property.

Soon after that, Rose answered the door to find the police with warrant in hand. She quickly called Fred to tell him the police were about to dig on their property and they're looking for Heather. It turned out that Fred would be of little help because it took him four hours to get home. He came up with some excuse about passing out due to inhaling paint fumes at work.

Could it have been that Fred was busy disposing of evidence such as fingers and toes or perhaps he had a burial he had not gotten around to completing. That will never be determined.

They began searching the house in addition to excavating the garden in February 24, 1994. The dig was originally intended to search for the body of the daughter Heather, which they soon found. Fred was brought in by the police for questioning the next day. He surprised the police by confessing to the murder of his daughter Heather and he repeatedly told police that Rose knew nothing about it.

Fred and Rose must have been up all that night getting their stories straight. It is thought that Fred assured Rose he would take all the blame and she shouldn't worry. Fred was good to his word, at least in the beginning.

Meanwhile, after the attending pathologist began inspecting the bones of Heather, he brought it to the attention of the police that there was an extra leg bone indicating the presence of at least one other body.

After that discovery, Fred decided he should do some damage control by telling police the location of Alison Chambers and Shirley Robinson's bodies. He hoped this would prevent them from doing any more digging.

It was first thought that Fred did this to avoid being categorized a serial killer, which is someone that kills more than three people. Unbelievably, as it turned out, Fred wanted the police to stop digging because he didn't want his cherished home to be torn apart any further.

Nevertheless, they continued and began to find more human bones. Rose was not arrested until around March 4, 1994. Even then, it was only for sex offenses. Fred had trouble deciding for sure if he wanted to protect Rose after all. He would go on the recant his confession that he killed Heather and then later changed his mind again saying Rose was innocent.

In Britain, prisoners are sometimes assigned an "appropriate adult", which is someone that assists and basically befriends the prisoner. This was normally done for juveniles; however, Janet Leach was assigned to Fred. Leach didn't know she was about to become the confidant of a serial killer.

It turned out that Fred became comfortable enough with Leach that he soon told her the whole gory story. She pointblank asked him if there were more victims. Fred responded that there were six more and went on to draw a sketch of his house and garden complete with the locations of the graves.

Fred knew exactly where they were located; however, he had some trouble remembering all their names. He recalled one that had a scar on her hand; therefore, Scar Hand became her name. Another he called Tulip because he thought she was Dutch, although she was actually Swiss.

Fred was now on a roll and confessed to the murders of his ex-wife Rena Costello and ex-lover, Anne McFall. He told leach that he dumped them nearby his childhood home. He then confessed that he buried his step-daughter Charmaine, Fred's child that Rose killed, close to the hotel where they lived in Gloucester. Strangely, Fred would admit to the murders, but he would not admit to the rapes.

Meanwhile, Rose continued to play the role of an innocent woman, denying any involvement in the murders. She went so far as to act horrified at the actions of her perverted husband. When Fred attempted to contact her, she snubbed him not wanting to have anything to do with such a despicable person.

After making bail, Rose moved into a halfway house with her son Stephen and her daughter Mae. The police were not convinced of her innocence and bugged the house. Nevertheless, Rose stuck to it and never spoke of anything that would involve her in murder. Only charges of sexual offense remained against her.

As can be imagined, the town of Gloucester was flooded with the media. The attention had a tremendous impact on the small town. The West's house became known by the appropriate name "The House of Horrors". The residents were in disbelief that this unimaginable crime spree had gone on in their town for 20 years.

The Trial

As it turned out, Fred took the easy way out. He hanged himself in his jail cell by tying together bed sheets leaving Rose to deal with the whole state of affairs.

She was finally charged with 10 of the murders since Rena Costello and Anne McFall were before she was on the scene. She went to trial in October of 1995.

One after another, witnesses took the stand and told their shocking stories. One of the highest drama moments of the trial came with the testimony of Fred's oldest daughter, Anna Marie. She was on the stand for two days. At one point she looked her stepmother straight in the eye as she told a story of sexual abuse and torture that began when she was a little girl of only eight-years-old.

She recalled the incident when she was so savagely raped by her father while Rose held her arms. During the incident, Rose was telling her how lucky she was to have parents to show her how to please her husband when she gets married. She said she was hurt so badly that she couldn't attend school for several days. She also recalled a day that her father strapped her down and raped her while he was home for a quick lunch break. These were only two of the many horror stories she lived.

The second day of her testimony was delayed for several hours because she took an overdose of pills the previous evening.

Another person that offered a wealth of damaging testimony was Fred's *Appropriate Adult* and confidant, Janet Leach. However, she became so stressed that she suffered a stroke during the trial causing another delay. It wasn't until later after the trial's end that Leach could tell police the entire story that Fred confided in her.

One of the key witnesses was Carol Owens who was one of the girls they brought home under the pretense of being a nanny. She was allowed to leave, but only after she endured their sadistic sexual torture. Needless to say, she had tales to tell.

Another witness who is still referred to as Miss A was lured to the West house and saw two naked girls who were being held prisoner. She watched as they were tortured and raped. She was then raped by Fred and sexually assaulted by Rose. She was one of the lucky ones that left that cellar with her life.

It wasn't hard for the jury to come back with a unanimous verdict of guilty on 10 counts of murder. Rose received life in prison.

The Aftermath

The "House of Horrors" at 25 Cromwell Street in Gloucester where nine bodies were found was demolished in October of 1996; however, there seemed to be a curse that affected many of the people associated with Rose and Fred West.

John West, Fred's brother, hanged himself while awaiting his trial for the rape of his own niece Anna Marie.

Anna Marie continued to suffer from the memories of her distorted childhood. In 1999, she attempted suicide by jumping from a bridge. She was rescued, leaving her to live another day with the memory of the horrors from her past.

Stephen West, the son of Rose and Fred, attempted to commit suicide in 2002 in the same manner as his father and uncle by hanging himself. However, it wasn't meant to be because the rope broke.

The actual number of murders will remain a mystery. During his interrogation by the police, Fred stated that there were two more bodies buried in shallow graves that they would never find.

He also told them there were 20 other bodies spread around in various places. He claimed he would show the police the location of one body each year. One wonders if he knew at that time that he would later take his own life and wouldn't be following through with that promise.

Fred took any other secrets he had in his evil little mind with him to his grave. After that, Rose wasn't interested in discussing the matter any further.

According to an article in the DailyMail, dated February 2014, even though Rose West filed for a couple of appeals after she went to prison, she has now decided she never wants to leave her top security jail cell at Low Newton jail in Durham and why would she, her cell is equipped with TV, radio, CD player, and private bathroom. She has never confessed to committing any murders.

Authorities know the women and girls were tortured, raped, killed, dismembered, and buried; however, they don't know the details of many of those crimes. Rose has been asked by numerous people to give those details, but she refuses.

Conclusion

This is an account of actual facts; however, it hard to believe that it's anything other than a fictional horror story.

Even after hearing about the disturbing childhoods of both Rose and Fred West, it's difficult to understand the extent of their warped minds. Even more disturbing is the fact that two people that are this broken can find one another and carry out their evil deeds together.

This story brings us no closer to the answer of what drives serial killers. Both Rose and Fred were abused as children mainly by their fathers; however, it was young women and girls that were the focus of their punishment.

There have been books and a movie made about them to show us how this horrific story unfolds. However, only in our minds can we come close to conjuring up the evil that occurred within the walls of 25 Cromwell Street. We may never know the full extent of the terrors that transpired.

The fact that Fred West is gone and Rose West will never see the light of day should make us all sleep a little more soundly.